CALVIN ON REPENTANCE

A continual process of transformation.

JOHN CALVIN
CALEB SINCLAIR

Published by
GRAPEVINE BOOKS

www.grapevinebooks.com
email: contact@grapevinebooks.com

Ordering Information:
Quantity sales: Special discounts are available on quantity purchases
by corporations, associations, and others.
For details, reach out to the publisher.

First published by Grapevine Books, 2025

I

Though we have already shown, in some respect, how faith possesses Christ, and how by means of faith we enjoy his benefits, yet the subject would still be involved in obscurity, unless we were to add a description of the effects which we experience. The substance of the gospel is, not without reason, said to be comprised in "repentance and remission of sins." Therefore, if these two points be omitted, every controversy concerning faith will be jejune and incomplete, and consequently of little use. Now, since both are conferred on us by Christ, and we obtain both by faith,—that is, newness of life and gratuitous reconciliation,—the regular method of instruction requires me, in this place, to enter on the discussion of both. But our immediate transition will be from faith to repentance; because, when this point is well understood, it will better appear how man is justified by faith alone, and mere pardon, and yet that real sanctity of life (so to speak) is not separated from the gratuitous imputation of righteousness. Now, it ought not to be doubted that repentance not only immediately follows faith, but is produced by it. For since pardon, or remission, is offered by the preaching of the gospel, in order that the sinner, liberated from the tyranny of Satan, from the yoke of sin, and the miserable servitude of his vices, may remove into the kingdom of God,—no one can embrace the grace of the gospel, but he must depart from the errors of his former life, enter into the right way, and devote all his attention to the exercise of repentance. Those who imagine that repentance rather precedes faith, than is produced by it, as fruit by a tree, have never been acquainted with its power, and are induced to adopt that sentiment by a very insufficient argument.

II.

They argue that Jesus Christ and John the Baptist, in their preaching, first exhort the people to repentance; and afterwards add, that "the kingdom of heaven is at hand;" that thus the apostles were commanded to preach, and that this (according to the account of Luke) was the method followed by Paul. But they superstitiously attend to the connection of the syllables, and disregard the sense and coherence of the words. For when Christ and John preach in this manner, "Repent, for the kingdom of heaven is at hand," do they not derive an argument for repentance from grace itself, and the promise of salvation? The meaning of their language, therefore, is just as though they had said, Since the kingdom of heaven is at hand, therefore repent. For Matthew, having related that John preached in this

manner, informs us, that in him was accomplished the prediction of Isaiah concerning "the voice of one crying in the wilderness, Prepare ye the way of the Lord, make his paths straight." But, in the prophet, that voice is commanded to begin with consolation and glad tidings. Yet, when we speak of faith as the origin of repentance, we dream not of any space of time which it employs in producing it; but we intend to signify, that a man cannot truly devote himself to repentance, unless he knows himself to be of God. Now, no man is truly persuaded that he is of God, except he has previously received his grace. But these things will be more clearly discussed as we proceed. This circumstance, perhaps, has deceived them—that many are overcome or led to obedience by terrors of conscience, before they have imbibed a knowledge of grace, or have even tasted it. And this is the initial fear, which some number among the graces, because they perceive it to be nearly connected with true and righteous obedience. But we are not inquiring, at present, in how many ways Christ draws us to himself, or prepares us for the practice of piety: only I assert, that no rectitude can be found but where that Spirit reigns, whom he has received in order to communicate him to his members. In the next place, according to this passage in the Psalms, "There is forgiveness with thee, that thou mayest be feared," no man will ever reverence God, but he who confides in his being propitious to him: no man will cheerfully devote himself to the observance of his law, but he who is persuaded that his services are pleasing to him: and this indulgence in pardoning us, and bearing with our faults, is an evidence of his paternal favour. The same also appears from this exhortation of Hosea, "Come, and let us return unto the Lord; for he hath torn, and he will heal us; he hath smitten, and he will bind us up;" because the hope of pardon is added as a stimulus, to prevent them from being stupefied in their sins. But there is not the least appearance of reason in the notion of those who, in order to begin with repentance, prescribe to their young converts certain days, during which they must exercise themselves in repentance; after the expiration of which, they admit them to the communion of evangelical grace. I speak of many of the Anabaptists, especially of those who wonderfully delight in being accounted spiritual; and their companions, the Jesuits, and other such worthless men. Such are the effects produced by that spirit of fanaticism, that it terminates repentance within the limits of a few short days, which a Christian ought to extend throughout his whole life.

III.

But concerning repentance, some learned men, in times very remote from the present, desiring to express themselves with simplicity and sincerity according to the rule of the Scripture, have said that it consists of two parts—mortification and vivification. Mortification they explain to be the sorrow of the mind, and the terror experienced from a knowledge of sin and a sense of the Divine judgments. For when any one has been brought to a true knowledge of sin, he then begins truly to hate and abhor it; then he is heartily displeased with himself, confesses himself to be miserable and lost, and wishes that he were another man. Moreover, when he is affected with some sense of the Divine judgment, (for the one immediately follows the other,) then, indeed, he is stricken with consternation, he trembles with humility and dejection, he feels a despondency of mind, he falls into despair. This is the first part of repentance, which they have generally styled contrition. Vivification they explain to be the consolation which is produced by faith; when a man, after having been humbled with a consciousness of sin, and stricken with the fear of God, afterwards contemplates the goodness of God, and the mercy, grace, and salvation bestowed through Christ, rises from his depression, feels himself re-invigorated, recovers his courage, and as it were returns from death to life. These terms, provided they be rightly understood, are sufficiently adapted to express the nature of repentance; but when they explain vivification of that joy which the mind experiences after its perturbations and fears are allayed, I cannot coincide with them; since it should rather signify an ardent desire and endeavour to live a holy and pious life, as though it were said, that a man dies to himself, that he may begin to live to God.

IV

Others, perceiving this word to have various acceptations in Scripture, have laid down two kinds of repentance; and, to distinguish them by some character, have called one Legal; in which the sinner, wounded by the envenomed dart of sin, and harassed by the fear of Divine wrath, is involved in deep distress, without the power of extricating himself: the other they style Evangelical; in which the sinner is grievously afflicted in himself, but rises above his distress, and embraces Christ as the medicine for his wound, the consolation of his terrors, and his refuge from all misery.

Of legal repentance, they consider Cain, Saul, and Judas, as examples; the scriptural account of whose repentance gives us to understand, that from a knowledge of the greatness of their sins they dreaded the Divine wrath, but that considering God only as an avenger and a judge, they perished under that apprehension. Their repentance, therefore, was only, as it were, the antechamber of hell, which having already entered in this life, they began to suffer punishment from the manifestation of the wrath of the Divine Majesty. Evangelical repentance we discover in all who have been distressed by a sense of sin in themselves, but have been raised from their depression, and reinvigorated by a confidence in the Divine mercy, and converted to the Lord. Hezekiah was terrified when he received the message of death; but he wept and prayed, and, contemplating the goodness of God, recovered his former confidence. The Ninevites were confounded by the terrible denunciation of destruction; but they covered themselves with sackcloth and ashes, and prayed, in hope that the Lord might be appeased, and the fury of his wrath averted. David confessed that he had committed a great sin in numbering the people; but added, "O Lord, take away the iniquity of thy servant." He acknowledged his crime of adultery at the rebuke of Nathan, and prostrated himself before the Lord; but at the same time cherished an expectation of pardon. Such was the repentance of those who felt compunction of heart at the preaching of Peter, but, confiding in the goodness of God, exclaimed, "Men and brethren, what shall we do?" Such also was that of Peter himself, who wept bitterly, but never lost his hope.

V

Though all these observations are true, yet the term repentance, as far as I can ascertain from the Scriptures, must have a different acceptation. For to include faith in repentance, is repugnant to what Paul says in the Acts—that he testified "both to the Jews, and also to the Greeks, repentance toward God, and faith toward our Lord Jesus Christ;" where he mentions faith and repentance, as two things totally distinct. What then? Can true repentance exist without faith? Not at all. But though they cannot be separated, yet they ought to be distinguished. As faith exists not without hope, and yet there is a difference between them, so repentance and faith, although they are perpetually and indissolubly united, require to be connected rather than confounded. I am well aware, that under the term repentance is comprehended a complete conversion to God, of which faith is one of the principal branches; but in what sense, will best appear

from an explication of its nature and properties. The Hebrew word for repentance denotes conversion or return. The Greek word signifies change of mind and intention. Repentance itself corresponds very well with both etymologies, for it comprehends these two things—that, forsaking ourselves, we should turn to God, and laying aside our old mind, should assume a new one. Wherefore I conceive it may be justly defined to be "a true conversion of our life to God, proceeding from a sincere and serious fear of God, and consisting in the mortification of our flesh and of the old man, and in the vivification of the Spirit." In this sense we must understand all the addresses, in which either the prophets in ancient days, or the apostles in a succeeding age, exhorted their contemporaries to repentance. For the point to which they endeavoured to bring them was this—that being confounded by their sins, and penetrated with a fear of the Divine judgment, they might prostrate themselves in humility before him against whom they had offended, and with true penitence return into his right way. Therefore these expressions, "to repent" and "to return to the Lord," are promiscuously used by them in the same signification. Hence also the sacred history expresses repentance by seeking after and following God, when men who have disregarded him, and indulged their criminal propensities, begin to obey his word, and are ready to follow whithersoever he calls them. And John and Paul have spoken of "bringing forth fruits meet for repentance," to signify a life which, in every action, will discover and testify such a repentance.

VI

But before we proceed any further, it will be useful to amplify and explain the definition we have given; in which there are three points to be particularly considered. In the first place, when we call repentance "a conversion of the life to God," we require a transformation, not only in the external actions, but in the soul itself; which, after having put off its old nature, should produce the fruits of actions corresponding to its renovation. The prophet, intending to express this idea, commands those whom he calls to repentance, to make themselves a new heart. Wherefore Moses, when about to show how the Israelites might repent and be rightly converted to the Lord, frequently teaches them that it must be done with all their heart, and with all their soul; and by speaking of the circumcision of the heart, he enters into the inmost affections of the mind. This mode of expression we find often repeated by the prophets; but there is no passage from which we may obtain clearer ideas of the true nature of repentance, than from the language of God in the fourth Chapter of Jeremiah: "If thou wilt return, O Israel, saith the Lord, return unto me. Break up your fallow ground, and sow not among thorns. Circumcise yourselves to the Lord, and take away the foreskins of your heart." Observe how he denounces that they shall labour in vain in the pursuit of righteousness, unless impiety be previously eradicated from the bottom of their hearts. And in order to make a deeper impression upon them, he apprizes them that they have to do with God, with whom subterfuges are of no avail, because he abhors all duplicity of heart. For this reason, Isaiah ridicules the preposterous endeavours of hypocrites, who did indeed strenuously attempt an external repentance by the observance of ceremonies, but at the same time were not concerned "to loose the bands of wickedness," with which they oppressed the poor. In that passage he also beautifully shows, in what duties unfeigned repentance properly consists.

VII

In the second place, we represented repentance as proceeding from a serious fear of God. For before the mind of a sinner can be inclined to repentance, it must be excited by a knowledge of the Divine judgment. But when this thought has once been deeply impressed, that God will one day ascend his tribunal to exact an account of all words and actions, it will not permit the miserable man to take any interval of rest, or to enjoy even a momentary respite, but perpetually stimulates him to adopt a new course of life, that he may be able to appear with security at that judgment. Wherefore the Scripture, when it exhorts to repentance, frequently introduces a mention of the judgment; as in Jeremiah; "Lest my fury come forth like fire, and burn that none can quench it, because of the evil of your doings:" in the address of Paul to the Athenians; "The times of this ignorance God winked at; but now commandeth all men every where to repent; because he hath appointed a day in which he will judge the world in righteousness:" and in many other places. Sometimes, by the punishments already inflicted, it declares that God is a judge; in order that sinners may consider with themselves that worse calamities await them, unless they speedily repent. We have an example of this in the twenty-ninth Chapter of Deuteronomy. But since conversion commences with a dread and hatred of sin, therefore the apostle makes godly sorrow the cause of repentance. He calls it godly sorrow when we not only dread punishment, but hate and abhor sin itself, from a knowledge that it is displeasing to God. Nor ought this to be thought strange; for, unless we felt sharp compunction, our carnal sluggishness could never be corrected, and even these distresses of mind would not be sufficient to arouse it from its stupidity and indolence, if God, by the infliction of his chastisements, did not make a deeper impression. Beside this, there is a rebellious obstinacy, which requires violent blows, as it were, to overcome it. The severity, therefore, which God uses in his threatenings, is extorted from him by the depravity of our minds; since it would be in vain for him to address kind and alluring invitations to those who are asleep. I forbear to recite the testimonies with which the Scripture abounds. The fear of God is called the beginning of repentance also for another reason; because though a man's life were perfect in every virtue, if it be not devoted to the worship of God, it may indeed be commended by the world, but in heaven it will be only an abomination; since the principal branch of righteousness consists in rendering to God the honour due to him, of which he is impiously defrauded, when it is not our end and aim to submit ourselves to his government.

VIII

It remains for us, in the third place, to explain our position, that repentance consists of two parts—the mortification of the flesh and the vivification of the spirit. This is clearly expressed by the prophets, although in a simple and homely manner, according to the capacity of a carnal people, when they say, "Depart from evil, and do good." Again: "Wash you, make you clean; put away the evil of your doings from before mine eyes; cease to do evil; learn to do well; seek judgment; relieve the oppressed," &c. For when they call men from the paths of wickedness, they require the total destruction of the flesh, which is full of wickedness and perverseness. It is a thing truly difficult and arduous to put off ourselves, and to depart from the native bias of our minds. Nor must the flesh be considered as entirely dead, unless all that we have of ourselves be destroyed. But since the universal disposition of the flesh is settled "enmity against God," the first step to an obedience of the law is this renunciation of our own nature. They afterwards designate the renovation by its fruits—righteousness, judgment, and mercy. For a punctual performance of these external duties would not be sufficient, unless the mind and heart had previously acquired a disposition of righteousness, judgment, and mercy. This takes place when the Spirit of God has tinctured our souls with his holiness, and given them such new thoughts and affections, that they may be justly considered as new, [or altogether different from what they were before.] And certainly, as we have a natural aversion to God, we shall never aim at that which is right, without a previous renunciation of ourselves. Therefore we are so frequently commanded to put off the old man, to renounce the world and the flesh, to forsake our lusts, and to be renewed in the spirit of our mind. Besides, the very word mortification reminds us how difficult it is to forget our former nature; for it implies that we cannot be formed to the fear of God, and learn the rudiments of piety, without being violently slain and annihilated by the sword of the Spirit. As though God had pronounced that, in order to our being numbered among his children, there is a necessity for the destruction of our common nature.

IX

Both these branches of repentance are effects of our participation of Christ. For if we truly partake of his death, our old man is crucified by its power, and the body of sin expires, so that the corruption of our former nature loses all its vigour. If we are partakers of his resurrection, we are raised by it to a newness of life, which corresponds with the righteousness of God. In one word I apprehend repentance to be regeneration, the end of which is the restoration of the Divine image within us; which was defaced, and almost obliterated, by the transgression of Adam. Thus the apostle teaches us, when he says, "But we all, with open face beholding as in a glass the glory of the Lord, are changed into the same image from glory to glory, even as by the Spirit of the Lord." Again: "Be ye renewed in the spirit of your mind; and put on the new man, which after God is created in righteousness and true holiness." Again, in another place: "And ye have put on the new man, which is renewed in knowledge after the image of him that created him." Wherefore, in this regeneration, we are restored by the grace of Christ to the righteousness of God, from which we fell in Adam; in which manner the Lord is pleased completely to restore all those whom he adopts to the inheritance of life. And this restoration is not accomplished in a single moment, or day, or year; but by continual, and sometimes even tardy advances, the Lord destroys the carnal corruptions of his chosen, purifies them from all pollution, and consecrates them as temples to himself; renewing all their senses to real purity, that they may employ their whole life in the exercise of repentance, and know that this warfare will be terminated only by death. And so much the greater is the wickedness of that impure and quarrelsome apostate Staphylus, who idly pretends that I confound the state of the present life with the glory of heaven, when I explain the image of God, according to Paul, to be righteousness and true holiness. As if, indeed, when any thing is to be defined, we are not to inquire after the completeness and perfection of it. It is not denied that there is room for further advances; but I assert, that as far as any man approaches to a resemblance of God, so far the image of God is displayed in him. That believers may attain to this, God assigns them the race of repentance to run during their whole life.

X

Thus, therefore, the children of God are liberated by regeneration from the servitude of sin; not that they have already obtained the full possession of liberty, and experience no more trouble from the flesh, but there remains in them a perpetual cause of contention to exercise them; and not only to exercise them, but also to make them better acquainted with their own infirmity. And on this subject all sound writers are agreed—that there still remains in a regenerate man a fountain of evil, continually producing irregular desires, which allure and stimulate him to the commission of sin. They acknowledge, also, that saints are still so afflicted with the disease of concupiscence, that they cannot prevent their being frequently stimulated and incited either to lust, or to avarice, or to ambition, or to other vices. There is no need of a laborious investigation, to learn what were the sentiments of the fathers on this subject: it will be sufficient to consult Augustine alone, who with great diligence and fidelity has collected the opinions of them all. From him, then, the reader may receive all the certainty he can desire concerning the sense of antiquity. Between him and us, this difference may be discovered—that while he concedes that believers, as long as they inhabit a mortal body, are so bound by concupiscence that they cannot but feel irregular desires, yet he ventures not to call this disease by the name of sin, but, content with designating it by the appellation of infirmity, teaches that it only becomes sin in cases where either action or consent is added to the conception or apprehension of the mind, that is, where the will yields to the first impulse of appetite. But we, on the contrary, deem it to be sin, whenever a man feels any evil desires contrary to the Divine law; and we also assert the depravity itself to be sin, which produces these desires in our minds. We maintain, therefore, that sin always exists in the saints, till they are divested of the mortal body; because their flesh is the residence of that depravity of concupiscence, which is repugnant to all rectitude. Nevertheless, he has not always refrained from using the word sin in this sense; as when he says, "Paul gives the appellation of sin to this, from which all sins proceed, that is, to carnal concupiscence. This, as it respects the saints, loses its kingdom on earth, and has no existence in heaven." In these words he acknowledges that believers are guilty of sin, inasmuch as they are the subjects of carnal concupiscence.

XI

But when God is said "to cleanse his church" from all sin, to promise the grace of deliverance in baptism, and to fulfil it in his elect,—we refer these phrases rather to the guilt of sin, than to the existence of sin. In the regeneration of his children, God does indeed destroy the kingdom of sin in them, (for the Spirit supplies them with strength, which renders them victorious in the conflict;) but though it ceases to reign, it continues to dwell in them. Wherefore we say, that "the old man is crucified," that the law of sin is abolished in the children of God, yet so that some relics remain; not to predominate over them, but to humble them with a consciousness of their infirmity. We grant, indeed, that they are not imputed, any more than if they did not exist; but we likewise contend that it is owing to the mercy of God that the saints are delivered from this guilt, who would otherwise be justly accounted sinners and guilty before him. Nor will it be difficult for us to confirm this opinion, since there are clear testimonies of Scripture to support it. What can we desire more explicit than the declaration of Paul to the Romans? In the first place, that he there speaks in the character of a regenerate man, we have already shown; and Augustine has evinced the same by the strongest arguments. I say nothing of his using the words evil and sin. However those who wish to oppose us may cavil at those words, yet who can deny that a resistance to the Divine law is evil? who can deny that an opposition to righteousness is sin? finally, who will not admit that there is guilt wherever there is spiritual misery? But all these things are affirmed by Paul respecting this disease. Besides, we have a certain demonstration from the law, by which this whole question may be briefly decided. For we are commanded to love God with all our heart, with all our mind, and with all our strength. Since all the powers of our soul ought to be thus occupied by the love of God, it is evident that the precept is not fulfilled by those who receive into their hearts the least desire, or admit into their minds any thought, which may draw them aside from the love of God into vanity. What then? Are not these properties of the soul,—to be affected with sudden emotions, to apprehend in the sensory, and to form conceptions in the mind? When these, therefore, open a way for the admission of vain and corrupt thoughts, do they not show that they are so far destitute of the love of God? Whoever, therefore, refuses to acknowledge that all the inordinate desires of the flesh are sins, and that

that malady of concupiscence, which they call an incentive to sin, is the source of sin, must necessarily deny the transgression of the law to be sin.

XII

If it be thought absurd, that all the natural appetites of man should be thus universally condemned, since they were implanted by God, the author of nature,—we reply, that we by no means condemn those desires, which God implanted so deeply in the nature of man at his first creation that they cannot be eradicated from it without destroying humanity itself, but only those insolent and lawless appetites which resist the commands of God. But now, since, through the depravity of nature, all its powers are so vitiated and corrupted, that disorder and intemperance are visible in all our actions; because the appetites are inseparable from such excesses, therefore we maintain that they are corrupt. Or, if it be wished to have the substance of our opinion in fewer words, we say, that all the desires of men are evil; and we consider them to be sinful, not as they are natural, but because they are inordinate; and we affirm they are inordinate, because nothing pure or immaculate can proceed from a corrupted and polluted nature. Nor does Augustine deviate from this doctrine so much as he appears to do. When he is too much afraid of the odium with which the Pelagians endeavoured to overwhelm him, he sometimes refrains from using the word sin: yet when he says, "that the law of sin remains in the saints, and that only the guilt is abolished," he sufficiently indicates that he is not averse to our opinion.

XIII

We will adduce some other passages, from which his sentiments will more fully appear. In his second book against Julian: "This law of sin is both abolished in the spiritual regeneration, and continues in the mortal flesh; abolished, since the guilt is removed in the sacrament, by which believers are regenerated; but continues, because it produces those desires against which also believers contend." Again: "Therefore the law of sin, which was in the members even of so great an apostle, is abolished in baptism, but not finally destroyed." Again: "The law of sin, the remaining guilt of which is removed in baptism, Ambrose has called iniquity; because it is iniquitous for the flesh to lust against the spirit." Again: "Sin is dead in that guilt in which it held us; and, although dead, it will rebel till it is cured by the perfection of burial." In the fifth book, he is still more explicit: "As blindness of heart is both a sin, which consists in a man's not believing in God; and a punishment for sin, by which a proud heart is deservedly punished; and also a cause of sin, when any is committed through the error of a blind heart; so the concupiscence of the flesh, against which the good spirit lusteth, is both a sin, because it is a disobedience against the government of the mind; and a punishment for sin, because it is inflicted for the demerits of the disobedient; and also a cause of sin, consenting by defection, or produced from contagion." Here he styles it sin, without any ambiguity; because, having overthrown error and confirmed the truth, he is not so much afraid of calumnies; as also in the forty-first homily on John, where he undoubtedly speaks the real sentiments of his mind: "If in the flesh you serve the law of sin, do what the apostle himself says—'Let not sin reign in your mortal body, that ye should obey it in the lusts thereof.' He says not, let it not exist; but, let it not reign. As long as you live, sin must necessarily exist in your members; let it at least be divested of its kingdom, so that its commands may not be fulfilled." Those who contend that concupiscence is not sin, commonly object this passage of James—"When lust hath conceived, it bringeth forth sin." But this objection is easily repelled; for, unless we understand him there to speak of evil works exclusively, or of actual sins, even an evil volition cannot be accounted sin. But from his calling flagitious and criminal actions the offspring of lust, and attributing to them the name of sin, it does not necessarily follow that concupiscence is not an evil thing, and deserving of condemnation in the sight of God.

XIV

Some Anabaptists, in the present age, imagine I know not what frantic intemperance, instead of spiritual regeneration—that the children of God, being restored to a state of innocence, are no longer obliged to be solicitous to restrain the licentiousness of the flesh, but that they ought to follow the leadings of the Spirit, under whose direction it is impossible ever to err. It would be incredible that the mind of man should fall into such madness, did they not publicly and haughtily disseminate this opinion. It is indeed truly prodigious; but it is just and reasonable, that those who have persuaded themselves to pervert the truth of God into a falsehood, should suffer such punishment for their sacrilegious presumption. Must all distinction, then, of honour and turpitude, justice and injustice, good and evil, virtue and vice,

be annihilated? This difference, they say, proceeds from the malediction of the old Adam, from which we are delivered by Christ. Then there will be no difference now between chastity and fornication, sincerity and knavery, truth and falsehood, equity and rapine. Dismiss (they say) all vain fear; the Spirit will command you nothing that is evil, provided you securely and intrepidly resign yourself to his direction. Who is not astonished at these monstrous notions? Yet this is a popular philosophy among those, who, blinded by the violence of their appetites, have discarded common sense. But what kind of a Christ, and what kind of a Spirit, have they fabricated for us? For we acknowledge one Christ and his Spirit alone; whom the prophets have celebrated, whom the gospel proclaims as revealed, but of whom it gives us no such account as this. That Spirit is not the patron of murder, fornication, drunkenness, pride, contention, avarice, or fraud; but the author of love, chastity, sobriety, modesty, peace, moderation, and truth. He is not a Spirit of fanaticism, rushing precipitately, without any consideration, through right and wrong; but is full of wisdom and understanding, rightly to discern between justice and injustice. He never instigates to dissolute and unrestrained licentiousness; but, discriminating between what is lawful and what is unlawful, inculcates temperance and moderation. But why should we spend any more labour in refuting this monstrous frenzy? To Christians the Spirit of the Lord is not a turbulent phantom, which they have either spawned themselves in a dream, or received from the invention of others; but they religiously seek the knowledge of him in the Scriptures, where these two things are delivered concerning him—first, that he is given to us in order to our sanctification, to purify us from all our pollutions, and lead us to obey the Divine righteousness; which obedience cannot exist without the subjugation of the appetites, to which these men would allow an unlimited license: in the next place, that we are so purified by his sanctification, that we are nevertheless still encompassed with numerous vices and great infirmity, as long as we are burdened with the body. Wherefore, being at a great distance from perfection, it behoves us to make continual advances; and being entangled in vices, we have need to strive against them every day. Hence, also, it follows that we ought to shake off all slothful security, and exert the most vigilant attention, lest, without caution, we should be surprised and overcome by the snares of our flesh; unless we are well assured that we have made a greater progress than the apostle; who, nevertheless, was buffeted by the "messenger of Satan," that his strength might be "made perfect in weakness;" and who faithfully represented the conflict between the flesh and the Spirit, which he experienced in his own person.

XV

When the apostle, in a description of repentance, enumerates seven things, which are either causes producing it, or effects proceeding from it, or members and parts of it, he does it for a very good reason. These things are, carefulness, excuse, indignation, fear, vehement desire, zeal, revenge. Nor ought it to be thought strange that I venture not to determine whether they should be considered as causes or effects; for arguments may be adduced in support of both. They may also be styled affections connected with repentance; but as we may discover the meaning of Paul without discussing these questions, we shall be content with a simple exposition of them. He says, then, that godly sorrow produces solicitude. For a person who is affected with a serious sense of displeasure because he has sinned against his God, is at the same time stimulated to diligence and attention, that he may completely extricate himself from the snares of the devil, and be more cautious of his insidious attacks, that he may not in future disobey the government of the Spirit, or be overcome with a careless security. The next thing is self-excuse, which in this place signifies not a defence by which a sinner tries to escape the judgment of God, either by denying his transgressions or extenuating his guilt, but a kind of excuse, consisting rather in deprecation of punishment than in confidence of his cause. Just as children, who are not absolutely lost to all sense of duty, while they acknowledge and confess their faults, at the same time deprecate punishment, and, in order to succeed, testify by every possible method that they have not cast off that reverence which is due to their parents; in a word, they excuse themselves in such a manner, not to prove themselves righteous and innocent, but only to obtain pardon. This is followed by indignation, in which the sinner laments within himself, expostulates with himself, and is angry with himself, while he recollects his perverseness and ingratitude to God. The word fear denotes that trepidation with which our minds are penetrated, whenever we reflect upon our demerits, and on the terrible severity of the Divine wrath against sinners. For we cannot but be agitated with an amazing inquietude, which teaches us humility, and renders us more cautious for the future. Now, if the solicitude before mentioned be the offspring of fear, we see the connection and coherence between them. He appears to me to have used the word desire to denote diligence in duty and alacrity of obedience, to which the knowledge of our faults ought to be a most powerful stimulus. Similar to this is the meaning of zeal, which he immediately subjoins; for it signifies the ardour with which we are inflamed, when we are roused with such thoughts as these: "What have I done? Whither had I precipitated myself, if I had not been succoured by the mercy of God?" The last thing is revenge, or punishment; for the greater our severity is towards ourselves, and the stricter inquisition we make concerning our sins, so much the stronger hope ought we to entertain that God will be propitious and merciful. And, indeed, it is impossible but that a soul, impressed with a dread of the Divine judgment, must inflict some punishment on itself. Truly pious persons experience what punishments are contained in shame, confusion, lamentation, displeasure with themselves, and the other affections which arise from a serious acknowledgment of their transgressions. But let us remember that some limit must be observed, that we may not be overwhelmed in sorrow; for to nothing are terrified consciences more liable than to fall into despair. And with this artifice, also, whomsoever Satan perceives to be dejected by a fear of God, he plunges them further and further into the deep gulf of sorrow, that they may never arise again. That fear, indeed, cannot be excessive, which terminates in humility, and departs not from the hope of pardon. Nevertheless, the sinner should always be on his guard, according to the direction of the apostle,lest while he excites his heart to be displeased with himself, he be wearied with excessive dread, and faint in his mind; for this would drive us away from God, who calls us to himself by repentance. On this subject, Bernard also gives a very useful admonition: "Sorrow for sin is necessary, if it be not perpetual. I advise you sometimes to quit the anxious and painful recollection of your own ways, and to arise to an agreeable and serene remembrance of the Divine blessings. Let us mingle honey with wormwood, that its salutary bitterness may restore our health, when it shall be drunk tempered with a mixture of sweetness; and if you reflect on your own meanness, reflect also on the goodness of the Lord."

XVI

Now, it may also be understood what are the fruits of repentance. They are, the duties of piety towards God, and of charity towards men, with sanctity and purity in our whole life. In a word, the more diligently any one examines his life by the rule of the Divine law, so much the more certain evidences he discovers of his repentance. The Spirit, therefore, in frequently exhorting us to repentance, calls our attention, sometimes to all the precepts of the law, sometimes to the duties of the second table; though in other places, after having condemned impurity in the very fountain of the heart, he proceeds to those external testimonies which evidence a sincere repentance; a view of which I will soon exhibit to the reader, in a description of the Christian life. I shall not collect testimonies from the prophets, in which they partly ridicule the follies of those who attempt to appease God by ceremonies, and demonstrate them to be mere mockeries; and partly inculcate, that external integrity of life is not the principal branch of repentance, because God looks at the heart. He that is but ordinarily acquainted with the Scripture, will discover of himself, without being informed by any one, that in our concerns with God, we advance not a single step unless we begin with the internal affection of the heart. And this passage of Joel will afford us no small assistance in the interpretation of others: "Rend your heart, and not your garments." Both these ideas are briefly expressed in these words of James—"Cleanse your hands, ye sinners; and purify your hearts, ye double minded;" where there is indeed an addition made to the first clause; but the fountain, or original, is next discovered, showing the necessity of cleansing the secret pollution, that an altar may be erected to God even in the heart. There are likewise some external exercises which we use, in private, as remedies either to humble ourselves, or to subdue our carnality; and in public, to testify our repentance. They proceed from the revenge mentioned by Paul; for it is natural to an afflicted mind to continue in a squalid condition, groaning and weeping, to avoid every kind of splendour and pomp, and to forsake all pleasures. He who experiences the great evil of the rebellion of the flesh, seeks every remedy to restrain it. He who properly considers what a grievous thing it is to have offended the justice of God, can enjoy no repose till he has glorified God by his humility. Such exercises are frequently mentioned by the old writers, when they speak of the fruits of repentance. And though they by no means make repentance wholly to consist in them, yet the reader will pardon me if I deliver my opinion, that they appear to me to insist upon them more than they ought. And I hope every one, on a sober examination, will agree with me, that they have gone beyond all due bounds in two respects. For when they so strongly urged and so extravagantly recommended that corporeal discipline, the consequence was indeed that the common people adopted it with great ardour; but they also obscured that which ought to be esteemed of infinitely greater importance. Secondly, in the infliction of castigations, they used rather more rigour than was consistent with ecclesiastical gentleness. But we shall have to treat of this in another place.

XVII

But as some persons, when they find weeping, fasting, and ashes mentioned, not only in many other passages of Scripture, but particularly in Joel, consider fasting and weeping as the principal part of repentance, their mistake requires to be rectified. What is there said of the conversion of the whole heart to the Lord, and of rending not the garments, but the heart, properly belongs to repentance; but weeping and fasting are not added as perpetual or necessary effects of it, but as circumstances belonging to a particular case. Having prophesied that a most grievous destruction was impending over the Jews, he persuades them to prevent the Divine wrath, not only by repentance, but also by exhibiting external demonstrations of sorrow. For as it was customary, in ancient times, for an accused person to present himself in a suppliant posture, with a long beard, dishevelled hair, and mourning apparel, in order to conciliate the compassion of the judge, so it became those who stood as criminals before the tribunal of God, to deprecate his severity in a condition calculated to excite commiseration. Though sackcloth and ashes were perhaps more suitable to those times, yet it is evident that the practice of weeping and fasting would be very seasonable among us, whenever the Lord appears to threaten us with any affliction or calamity. For when he causes danger to appear, he, as it were, denounces that he is prepared and armed for the exercise of vengeance. The prophet, therefore, was right in exhorting his countrymen to weeping and fasting; that is, to the sadness of persons under accusation, into whose offences he had just before said that an examination was instituted. Neither would the pastors of the church act improperly in the present age, if, when they perceived calamity impending over the heads of their people, they called them to immediate weeping and fasting; provided they always insisted with the greatest fervour and diligence on the principal point, which is, that they must rend their hearts, and not their garments. It is certain, that fasting is not always the concomitant of repentance, but is appointed for times of peculiar calamity; wherefore Christ connects it with mourning, when he frees the apostles from any obligation to it, till they should be affected with grief at the loss of his presence. I speak of solemn fasting. For the life of the pious ought at all times to be regulated by frugality and sobriety, that through its whole progress it may appear to be a kind of perpetual fast. But as the whole of this subject must be discussed again, when we come to treat of Ecclesiastical Discipline, I touch the more slightly upon it at present.

XVIII

I will again remark, however, that when the word repentance is transferred to this external profession, it is improperly changed from the genuine signification which I have stated. For this external profession is not so much a conversion to God, as a confession of sin, with a deprecation of punishment and guilt. Thus to "repent in sackcloth and ashes," is only a declaration of our displeasure against ourselves, when God is angry with us on account of our grievous offences. And this is a public species of confession, by which condemning ourselves before angels and men, we prevent the judgment of God. For Paul rebukes the sluggishness of those who indulge their sins, saying, "If we would judge ourselves, we should not be judged." It is not necessary, in all cases, publicly to make men witnesses of our repentance; but a private confession to God is a branch of true penitence which cannot be omitted. For nothing is more unreasonable than that God should pardon sins, in which we encourage ourselves, and which, lest he should bring them to light, we conceal under the garb of hypocrisy. And it is not only necessary to confess the sins which we commit from day to day; more grievous falls ought to lead us further, and to recall to our remembrance those which appear to have been long buried in oblivion. We learn this from the example of David; for, being ashamed of a recent and flagitious crime, he examines himself back to the time of his conception, and acknowledges that even then he was corrupted and contaminated with carnal impurity; and this not to extenuate his guilt, as many conceal themselves in a multitude, and endeavour to escape with impunity by implicating others with themselves. Very different was the conduct of David, who ingenuously aggravated his guilt, by confessing that he was corrupted from his earliest infancy, and had never ceased to accumulate crimes upon crimes. In another place, also, he enters on such an examination of his past life, that he implores the Divine mercy to pardon the sins of his youth. And certainly we shall never give proof that we have shaken off our lethargy, till, groaning under the burden, and bewailing our misery, we pray to God for relief. It is further to be remarked, that the repentance which we are commanded constantly to practise, differs from that which arouses, as it were, from death those who have either fallen into some great enormity, or abandoned themselves to a course of sin with unrestrained license, or by any rebellion shaken off the Divine yoke. For when the Scripture exhorts to repentance, it frequently signifies a kind of transition and resurrection from death to life; and when it states that the people repented, it means that they departed from idolatry and other gross enormities; in which sense Paul declares his grief for sinners, who "have not repented of their uncleanness, and fornication, and lasciviousness." This difference should be carefully observed, lest, when we hear that few are called to repentance, we fall into a supine security, as though we had no more to do with the mortification of the flesh, from which the depraved appetites that perpetually disturb us, and the vices that often arise in us, will never permit us to relax. The special repentance, therefore, which is only required of some whom the devil has seduced from the fear of God, and entangled in his fatal snares, supersedes not that ordinary repentance, which the corruption of nature obliges us to practise during the whole course of our lives.

XIX

Now, if it be true, as it certainly is, that the whole substance of the gospel is comprised in these two points, repentance and remission of sins,—do not we perceive that the Lord freely justifies his children, that he may also restore them to true righteousness by the sanctification of his Spirit? John, the "messenger sent before the face" of Christ to "prepare his way before him," preached, "Repent ye, for the kingdom of heaven is at hand." By calling men to repentance, he taught them to acknowledge themselves to be sinners, and every thing belonging to them to be condemned before God, that they might earnestly desire and pray for a mortification of the flesh, and new regeneration in the Spirit. By announcing the kingdom of God, he called them to exercise faith; for by "the kingdom of God," the approach of which he proclaimed, he intended remission of sins, salvation, life, and in general all the benefits that we obtain in Christ. Wherefore, in the other evangelists, it is said, that "John came, preaching the baptism of repentance for the remission of sins." What was intended by this, but that, oppressed and wearied with the burden of sins, men should turn themselves to the Lord, and entertain a hope of remission and salvation? Thus, also, Christ commenced his public ministrations. "The kingdom of God is at hand: repent ye, and believe the gospel." First, he declares that the treasures of mercy are opened in himself; then he requires repentance; and lastly, a reliance on the Divine promises. Therefore, when he would give a brief summary of the whole gospel, he said, that "it behoved him to suffer, and to rise from the dead; and that repentance and remission of sins should be preached in his name." The apostles also, after his resurrection, preached that he was exalted by God, "to give repentance to Israel and remission of sins." Repentance is preached in the name of Christ, when men are informed, by the doctrine of the gospel, that all their thoughts, their affections, and their pursuits, are corrupt and vicious; and that therefore it is necessary for them to be born again, if they wish to enter the kingdom of God. Remission of sins is preached, when men are taught that Christ is made unto them "wisdom, and righteousness, and sanctification, and redemption;" in whose name they are gratuitously accounted righteous and innocent in the sight of God. Both these blessings of grace, as we have already shown, are apprehended by faith; yet since the goodness of God in the remission of sins is the peculiar object of faith, it was necessary that it should be carefully distinguished from repentance.

XX

Now, as a hatred of sin, which is the commencement of repentance, is our first introduction to the knowledge of Christ, who reveals himself to none but miserable and distressed sinners, who mourn, and labour, and are heavy laden; who hunger and thirst, and are pining away with grief and misery; so it is necessary for us, if we desire to abide in Christ, to strive for this repentance, to devote our whole lives to it, and to pursue it to the last. For he "came to call sinners," but it was to call them "to repentance." He was "sent to bless" the unworthy; but it was "in turning away every one from his iniquities." The Scripture is full of such expressions. Wherefore, when God offers remission of sins, he generally requires repentance on the part of the sinner; implying that his mercy ought to furnish a motive to excite us to repentance. "Keep ye judgment, and do justice; for my salvation is near." Again: "The Redeemer shall come to Zion, and unto them that turn from transgression in Jacob." Again: "Seek ye the Lord while he may be found, call ye upon him while he is near: let the wicked forsake his way, and the unrighteous man his thoughts; and let him return unto the Lord, and he will have mercy upon him." Again: "Repent, and be converted, that your sins may be blotted out." Here it must be remarked, however, that this condition is not annexed in such a manner, as though our repentance were the fundamental and meritorious cause of pardon; but rather, because the Lord has determined to have mercy upon men, in order that they may repent, he informs them what course they must take if they wish to obtain his favour. Therefore, as long as we inhabit the prison of our body, we shall have to maintain an incessant conflict with the vices of our corrupt nature, and even with our natural soul. Plato sometimes says, that the life of a philosopher is a meditation of death. We may assert with more truth, that the life of a Christian is perpetually employed in the mortification of

the flesh, till it is utterly destroyed, and the Spirit of God obtains the sole empire within us. Wherefore I think that he has made a very considerable proficiency, who has learned to be exceedingly displeased with himself: not that he should remain in this distress, and advance no further, but rather hasten and aspire towards God; that being ingrafted into the death and life of Christ, he may make repentance the object of his constant meditation and pursuit. And this cannot but be the conduct of those who feel a genuine hatred of sin; for no man ever hated sin, without having been previously captivated with the love of righteousness. This doctrine, as it is the most simple of all, so also it appears to me to be most consistent with the truth of the Scripture.

XXI

That repentance is a peculiar gift of God, must, I think, be so evident from the doctrine just stated, as to preclude the necessity of a long discourse to prove it. Therefore the Church praises and admires the goodness of God, that he "hath granted to the Gentiles repentance unto life;" and Paul, when he enjoins Timothy to be patient and gentle towards unbelievers, says, "If God, peradventure, will give them repentance, that they may recover themselves out of the snare of the devil." God affirms, indeed, that he wills the conversion of all men, and directs his exhortations promiscuously to all; but the efficacy of these exhortations depends on the Spirit of regeneration. For it were more easy to make ourselves men, than by our own power to endue ourselves with a more excellent nature. Therefore, in the whole course of regeneration, we are justly styled God's "workmanship, created unto good works, which God hath before ordained that we should walk in them." Whomsoever God chooses to rescue from destruction, them he vivifies by the Spirit of regeneration: not that repentance is properly the cause of salvation, but because, as we have already seen, it is inseparable from faith and the mercy of God; since, according to the testimony of Isaiah, "the Redeemer shall come to Zion, and unto them that turn from transgression in Jacob." It remains an unshaken truth, that wherever the fear of God prevails in the heart, the Spirit has operated to the salvation of that individual. Therefore, in Isaiah, where believers are bewailing and deploring their being deserted by God, they mention this as a sign of reprobation, that their hearts are hardened by him. The apostle also, intending to exclude apostates from all hope of salvation, asserts, as a reason, that "it is impossible to renew them again unto repentance;" because God, in the renewal of those whom he will not suffer to perish, discovers an evidence of his paternal favour, and attracts them to himself with the radiance of his serene and joyful countenance; whilst, on the contrary, he displays his wrath in hardening the reprobate, whose impiety is never to be forgiven. This kind of vengeance the apostle denounces against wilful apostates, who, when they depart from the faith of the gospel, deride God, contumeliously reject his grace, profane and trample on the blood of Christ, and do all in their power to crucify him again. For he does not, as is pretended by some preposterously severe persons, preclude all voluntary sinners from a hope of pardon. His design is to show that apostasy is unworthy of every excuse, and therefore it is not strange that God punishes such a sacrilegious contempt of himself with inexorable rigour. "For it is impossible (he tells us) for those who were once enlightened, and have tasted of the heavenly gift, and were made partakers of the Holy Ghost, and have tasted the good word of God, and the powers of the world to come, if they shall fall away, to renew them again unto repentance; seeing they crucify to themselves the Son of God afresh, and put him to an open shame." Again: "If we sin wilfully after that we have received the knowledge of the truth, there remaineth no more sacrifice for sins, but a certain fearful looking-for of judgment." These are the passages, from a misinterpretation of which the Novatians formerly derived a pretence for their extravagant opinions; and the apparent harshness of which has offended some good men, and induced them to believe that this Epistle is supposititious, though every part of it contains unequivocal evidences of the apostolic spirit. But as we are contending only with those who receive it, it is easy to show that these passages afford not the least countenance to their error. In the first place, the apostle must necessarily be in unison with his Master, who affirms that "all sin and blasphemy shall be forgiven unto men, but the blasphemy against the Holy Ghost, which shall not be forgiven, neither in this world, neither in the world to come." The apostle, I say, must certainly have been content with this exception, unless we wish to make him an enemy to the grace of Christ. Whence it follows, that pardon is denied to no particular sins, except one, which proceeds from desperate fury, and cannot be attributed to infirmity, but clearly proves a man to be possessed by the devil.

XXII

But, for the further elucidation of this subject, it is necessary to inquire into the nature of that dreadful crime which will obtain no forgiveness. Augustine somewhere defines it to be an obstinate perverseness, attended with a despair of pardon, and continued till death; but this is not consistent with the language of Christ, that "it shall not be forgiven in this world." For either this is a vain assertion, or the sin may be committed in this life. But if the definition of Augustine be right, it is never committed unless it continue till death. Others say, that a man sins against the Holy Ghost, who envies the grace bestowed on his brother. I know no foundation for this notion. But we will adduce the true definition; which when it shall have been proved by strong testimonies, will of itself easily overturn all others. I say, then, that the sin against the Holy Ghost is committed by those who, though they are so overpowered with the splendour of Divine truth that they cannot pretend ignorance, nevertheless resist it with determined malice, merely for the sake of resisting it. For Christ, in explanation of what he had asserted, immediately subjoins, "Whosoever speaketh a word against the Son of man, it shall be forgiven him; but whosoever speaketh against the Holy Ghost, it shall not be forgiven him." And Matthew, instead of "blasphemy against the Spirit," says, "blasphemy of the Spirit." How can any one cast a reproach on the Son, that is not also directed against the Spirit? Those who unadvisedly offend against the truth of God, which they know not, and who ignorantly revile Christ, but at the same time have such a disposition that they would not extinguish the Divine truth if revealed to them, or utter one injurious word against him whom they knew to be the Lord's Christ,—they sin against the Father and the Son. Thus there are many, in the present day, who most inveterately execrate the doctrines of the gospel, which if they knew to be the evangelical doctrine, they would be ready to venerate with their whole heart. But those who are convinced in their conscience, that it is the word of God which they reject and oppose, and yet continue their opposition,—they are said to blaspheme against the Spirit, because they strive against the illumination which is the work of the Holy Spirit. Such were some among the Jews, who, when they were not able to resist the Spirit that spake by Stephen, yet obstinately strove to resist. Many of them were undoubtedly urged to this conduct by a zeal for the law; but it appears that there were others, who were infuriated by a malignant impiety against God himself, that is, against the doctrine which they knew to be from God. Such also were the Pharisees, whom the Lord rebuked; who, in order to counteract the influence of the Holy Spirit, slanderously ascribed it to the power of Beelzebub. This, then, is "blasphemy of the Spirit," where the presumption of man deliberately strives to annihilate the glory of God. This is implied in the observation of Paul, that he "obtained mercy, because" he had "ignorantly in unbelief" committed those crimes, the demerits of which would otherwise have excluded him from the grace of the Lord. If the union of ignorance and

unbelief was the reason of his obtaining pardon, it follows that there is no room for pardon where unbelief has been attended with knowledge.

XXIII

But, on a careful observation, you will perceive that the apostle speaks not of one or more particular falls, but of the universal defection, by which the reprobate exclude themselves from salvation. We need not wonder that those whom John, in his canonical Epistle, affirms not to have been of the number of the elect from whom they departed, experience God to be implacable towards them. For he directs his discourse against those who imagined that they might return to the Christian religion, although they had once apostatized from it; to whom he contradicts this false and pernicious notion, declaring, what is absolutely true, that it is impossible for persons to return to the communion of Christ, who have knowingly and wilfully rejected it. And it is rejected, not by those who simply transgress the word of the Lord by a dissolute and licentious life, but by those who professedly renounce all his doctrines. Therefore the fallacy lies in the terms falling away and sinning; for the Novatians explain falling away to take place, when any one, after having been instructed by the law of the Lord that theft and fornication ought not to be committed, yet abstains not from either of these sins. But, on the contrary, I affirm that there is a tacit antithesis understood, which ought to contain a repetition of all the opposites of the things which had been previously mentioned; so that this passage expresses not any particular vice, but a universal defection from God, and if I may use the expression, an apostasy of the whole man. When he speaks, therefore, of some who fell away, "after they were once enlightened, and had tasted of the heavenly gift, and were made partakers of the Holy Ghost, and the powers of the world to come," it must be understood of persons who, with deliberate impiety, have smothered the light of the Spirit, rejected the taste of the heavenly gift, alienated themselves from the sanctification of the Spirit, and trampled on the word of God and the powers of the world to come. And the more fully to express that decided determination of impiety, he afterwards, in another place, adds the word wilfully. For when he says, that "if we sin wilfully after that we have received the knowledge of the truth, there remaineth no more sacrifice," he denies not that Christ is a perpetual sacrifice to expiate the iniquities of the saints, which almost the whole Epistle expressly proclaims in describing the priesthood of Christ, but intends that there remains no other where that is rejected. But it is rejected, when the truth of the gospel is avowedly renounced.

XXIV

The objection of some, who conceive it to be severe and inconsistent with the Divine clemency, that pardon should be refused to any who flee to the Lord imploring his mercy, is easily answered. For he affirms not that pardon is denied to them if they turn themselves to the Lord; but he absolutely denies the possibility of their attaining to repentance, because they are stricken with eternal blindness by the righteous judgment of God, on account of their ingratitude. Nor is it any objection that the same apostle afterwards accommodates to this subject the example of Esau, who vainly endeavoured with weeping and lamentation to recover his lost rights of primogeniture. Nor that the prophet utters this denunciation: "though they shall cry unto me, I will not hearken unto them." For such forms of expression signify neither true conversion nor invocation of God, but the anxiety felt by the impious in extreme calamity, which constrains them to consider, what before they carelessly disregarded, that nothing can do them any good but the assistance of the Lord. And this they do not so much implore, as bewail its being withheld from them. Therefore the prophet intends by crying, and the apostle by weeping, only that dreadful torment which excruciates the impious with the agonies of despair. This requires to be carefully observed, because otherwise this procedure of God would contradict his proclamation by the mouth of the prophet, that as soon as the sinner shall have turned, he will be propitious to him. And, as I have already remarked, it is certain that the human mind is not changed for the better, except by the previous influence of his grace. Nor will his promise respecting those who call upon him, ever deceive; but it is improper to apply the terms conversion and prayer to that blind torment by which the reprobate are distracted, when they see that it is necessary for them to seek God in order to find a remedy for their miseries, while at the same time they continue to flee from his approach.

XXV

But it is inquired, since the apostle denies that God is appeased by a hypocritical repentance, how Ahab obtained pardon, and averted the punishment with which he had been threatened, though he appears, from the subsequent tenor of his life, to have been only terrified by a sudden consternation. He clothed himself with sackcloth, sprinkled ashes upon his head, lay on the ground, and, as it is declared concerning him, "humbled himself before God;" but it was nothing to rend his garments, while his heart remained perverse and inflated with wickedness. Yet we see how God is inclined to clemency. I reply, that sometimes hypocrites are thus spared for a season, yet that the wrath of God always abides upon them, and that this is done not so much for their sakes, as for a public example. For what benefit did Ahab receive from the mitigation of the threatened punishment, but a respite from it during his continuance in this world? The malediction of God, therefore, although concealed, fixed itself in his family, and he himself went forward to eternal perdition. The same may be observed in the case of Esau; for though he suffered a repulse, yet a temporal benediction was granted to his tears. But since the spiritual inheritance, according to the oracle of God, could remain only with one of the brothers, when Jacob was chosen and Esau rejected, that preterition shut out the Divine mercy; yet this consolation was left to him as to a man on a level with the brutes, that he should be enriched with "the fatness of the earth and the dew of heaven." This is what I have just observed ought to be considered as an example to others, that we may learn to devote our minds and our exertions with more alacrity to sincere repentance; because it is not to be doubted that those who are truly and cordially converted will find God readily disposed to forgiveness, whose clemency extends itself even to the unworthy, as long as they manifest any appearance of contrition. At the same time, also, we are taught what dreadful vengeance awaits all the obstinate, who, with impudent countenances and hardened hearts, despise, disregard, and ridicule the Divine threatenings. Thus he frequently extended his hand to the children of Israel, to alleviate their distresses, notwithstanding their supplications were hypocritical, and their hearts full of duplicity and perfidy; as he complains in one of the Psalms, that they immediately after returned to their former courses. He designed by his merciful kindness, either to bring them to a serious conversion, or to render them inexcusable. Yet, by the temporary remission of punishments, he imposes on himself no perpetual law, but sometimes arises against hypocrites with the greater severity, and enhances their punishments, to manifest his extreme displeasure against hypocrisy. But he exhibits, as I have observed, some examples of his readiness to pardon, in order to animate the pious to a correction of their lives, and the more severely to condemn the pride of those who obstinately kick against the goads.

Note

If you wish to read more of this text, you can find it in Calvin's Institutes of the Christian Religion, Book III.

Repentance

John Calvin

Introduction

After discussing faith, let us now delve into the subject of repentance, for it is not only intricately joined together with faith, but also born out of it. As the gospel proclaims the divine grace and forgiveness to sinners, liberating them from the wretched shackles of sin and death, and ushering them into the kingdom of God, it becomes evident that one cannot truly receive the gospel's grace through faith without redirecting their wayward life and committing themselves earnestly to the contemplation and practice of genuine repentance.

There are those who argue, quite flippantly, that repentance precedes faith, rather than springing forth from it. They base this assertion on a rather literal interpretation, saying, "In their sermons, Christ and John first urge people to repentance, and then declare that the kingdom of God draws near. This same commandment was given to the apostles, and even St. Paul adhered to a similar order, as recounted by St. Luke" (Acts 17:30, 26:20). However, in their strict adherence to the sequential arrangement of words, they fail to grasp the underlying purpose of these statements and how they are intricately connected.

When Jesus Christ and John the Baptist issue the admonition, "Repent, for the kingdom of God is near" (Matthew 3:2, 4:17), are they not implying that repentance is caused by the fact that Jesus

Christ offers us grace and salvation? In essence, their words can be understood as follows: "Since the kingdom of God has drawn near, let us engage in repentance." Moreover, St. Matthew, in his account of John's preaching, asserts that it fulfills the prophecy of Isaiah, who spoke of a voice crying out in the wilderness, saying, "Prepare the way of the Lord, make straight His paths" (Matthew 3:3; Isaiah 40:3).

Therefore, it becomes clear that repentance is not a precursor to faith, but rather a natural outgrowth of it. It is the transformative response to the nearness of the kingdom of God, made possible through Jesus Christ. Behold, the prophet's decree states that the voice of repentance should commence with words of solace and joyful news.

Repentance in General

Yet, when we proclaim that faith is the source from which repentance springs, we do not suggest that it must endure a prolonged period of gestation. Rather, we seek to emphasize that one cannot truly embrace repentance until they recognize their belongingness to God. And how can one lay claim to belonging to God without first comprehending His boundless grace? However, the intricacies of this matter shall be expounded upon in the subsequent section.

Now, let us turn our attention to those who concoct a novel strain of Christianity, wherein certain days of repentance must be observed before one is deemed worthy of baptism and permitted to partake in the grace of the gospel. Alas! These proponents of error and madness, the self-proclaimed "spiritual" Anabaptists, fail to furnish any substantiation for their misguided notions. It is truly an unfortunate fruit borne by their deranged spirits—this notion of reserving a meager few days for repentance, a practice meant to span the entirety of a Christian's life.

Long ago, wise men endeavored to expound on repentance in its purest form, adhering strictly to the principles laid forth in scripture. They posited that repentance comprises two inseparable facets: mortification and vivification. They explained "mortification" as "a deep sorrow and fear of heart that arises from the realization of sin and the awareness of God's impending judgment." When one gains true insight into their transgressions, they cannot help but develop an aversion to sin. Indeed, they become displeased with themselves, confessing their wretchedness and shame, while harboring hope for transformation. Moreover, as this sense of impending judgment engulfs them (for the two are intertwined), they experience profound humility, terror, and a crushing weight of despair. They tremble and are disheartened, devoid of hope. This, my friends, is the initial stage of repentance, aptly referred to as "contrition."

The other facet, "vivification," is illuminated by the comforting embrace of faith. When an individual, plagued by the consciousness of their sin and gripped by the fear of God, directs their gaze towards His benevolence and mercy—contemplating the grace and salvation bestowed upon humanity through Jesus Christ—a transformative solace ensues. They find respite, their spirits rekindled, as they inhale the breath of life anew, transcending the grip of death itself.

Let these reflections resonate within our souls, for they bear the weight of theological contemplation. May our authoritative and didactic voice lead us to a place of reverence and introspection, as we embark on this deeply pastoral journey. Let us be stirred by the irony that lies subtly beneath the surface, and may these profound insights provoke thought, challenge preconceptions, and ultimately guide us towards profound spiritual enlightenment.

It is not uncommon for some to perceive two distinct forms of repentance, as they observe the varied ways in which the term is employed throughout scripture. To differentiate between them, they have labeled one as "legal" repentance, wherein the sinner, wounded by the searing agony of their transgressions and consumed by the terror of God's wrath, remains ensnared in a state of perpetual turmoil, unable to break free. The other kind of repentance they have dubbed "evangelical," for it is through this form that the sinner, despite being deeply afflicted within, rises to greater heights, embracing Jesus Christ as the cure for their ailment, the solace for their terror, and the savior from their wretchedness.

We find examples of legal repentance in the accounts of Cain, Saul, and Judas (Genesis 4:13-14; 1 Samuel 15:24-25, 30; Matthew 27:3- 4). Scripture depicts their repentance as a recognition of the weight of their sins and a fear of God's impending judgment. However, their focus remained fixed solely on divine retribution and the looming specter of judgment. Inevitably, they were overcome and their lives were ruined by this narrow perspective. Their repentance served as a gateway to perdition, leading them down a path to the torments of hell even in this present life, as they began to experience the wrath of God's majestic fury.

Conversely, we witness evangelical repentance in the lives of those who, despite being pierced to the core by the sting of sin, rise with confidence in the mercy of God and return to Him. Consider Hezekiah, who, upon receiving the message of his impending death, found himself distressed. Yet, he wept, prayed, and, contemplating God's mercy, gained renewed confidence (2 Kings 20:3; Isaiah 38:2ff). Similarly, the Ninevites were terror-stricken by the grave pronouncement of their imminent destruction. They clothed themselves in sackcloth and ashes, beseeching the Lord with prayers, hoping that His wrath might be turned away (Jonah 3:5-6). David, too, acknowledged his grievous sin of deceiving the people with a facade of righteousness. Nevertheless, he implored, "Lord, take away the sin of your servant" (2 Samuel 24:10). When confronted by the prophet Nathan,

David recognized the gravity of his transgressions, humbling himself before God and patiently awaiting forgiveness (2 Samuel 12:13). We witness this form of repentance in the hearts of those who were profoundly moved by the preaching of St. Peter, as they exclaimed, "What shall we do, brothers?" placing their trust in the goodness of God (Acts 2:37). The repentance of St. Peter himself is also of this nature, as he wept bitterly but never ceased to hope (Matthew 26:75; Luke 22:62).

Repentance More Deeply Understood

Let us deeply ponder these accounts, for they reveal the intricacies of theological contemplation. May our authoritative and didactic voice guide us on this journey of reverence and introspection, while embracing the profoundly pastoral tone that befits our quest for spiritual enlightenment. May the contemplation of these diverse forms of repentance provoke thought, challenge assumptions, and ultimately lead us to a place of profound spiritual growth and transformation.

Although these truths hold firm, it appears, based on my understanding of scripture, that we must apprehend the term "repentance" in a different light. It is rather amusing how some individuals conflate faith with repentance, despite the clear words of St. Paul in Acts, where he testifies of "repentance toward God and faith in Jesus Christ" as separate entities (Acts 20:21). Here, St. Paul himself distinguishes between faith and repentance. So, what shall we make of this? Can genuine repentance truly find its footing without faith? Absolutely not. While inseparable, they must be discerned as distinct. Just as faith cannot exist without hope, faith and hope are indeed separate entities. Similarly, repentance and faith, though bound together indissolubly, should be joined rather than confused. I am well aware that the term "repentance" encompasses the entire act of conversion to God, of which faith is a principal component. However, the precise nature and essence of repentance will become clear once we delve deeper into its characteristics. It is worth noting that the Hebrew term for repentance signifies "conversion," while the Greek equivalent denotes a "change of counsel and will." In truth, these terms align well with the essence of repentance itself. For at its core, repentance entails a turning away from ourselves and redirecting our gaze towards God. It necessitates forsaking our initial thoughts and wills, and embracing a new paradigm.

Therefore, in my discernment, it is fitting to define repentance in the following manner: it is an authentic conversion, a complete turnaround of our lives, leading us to wholeheartedly follow God and the path He reveals to us. Such a conversion springs forth from a genuine and unfeigned fear of God, which manifests itself in the mortification of our sinful nature and the vivification of the Spirit within us. This is the essence we must embrace when considering the numerous exhortations found in the writings of the prophets and apostles. Their intention is to guide the people of their time toward a state of repentance, urging them to feel a deep sense of shame for their transgressions and to be struck by the reverential fear of God's judgment. Through this humbling and prostration before the majesty of the offended God, they seek to realign individuals onto the right path. Hence, whenever they speak of turning back and returning to the Lord, of repenting and doing repentance, they always strive toward the same objective. St. Paul and St. John declare, "Let them produce fruits worthy of repentance" (Matthew 3:8; Acts 26:20; cf. Romans 6:4, 7:4–6). By this, they imply that a transformed life must bear witness to a genuine amendment in all its actions.

Three Views on Repentance

However, before we proceed any further, let us thoroughly unpack the aforementioned definition, which comprises three essential elements. Firstly, when we speak of repentance as a conversion of life to God, we demand more than mere external actions. We require a profound transformation within the depths of one's soul, wherein the old nature is stripped away, making room for the production of fruits worthy of this spiritual renewal. This notion finds resonance in the prophet's command for those he exhorts to repentance to possess a new heart. Even Moses, in his exhortation to the people of Israel regarding true conversion, repeatedly emphasizes the necessity to turn their hearts and souls wholly towards God. The prophets too employ this expression with great frequency (Ezekiel 18:30-31). However, it is in the fourth chapter of Jeremiah that we find a particularly illuminating passage through which we may grasp the true nature of repentance. There, God speaks in this manner: "Israel, if you turn, turn to me. Remove the evil of your deeds from before my eyes. Cease to do evil, learn to do good" (Jeremiah 4:1-4). Here, we witness the affirmation that in order to embark upon a path of righteousness, one must begin by uprooting all impiety from the depths of the heart. It is for this reason that Isaiah mocks the hollow endeavors of the hypocrites in his time, who sought to reform their lives externally, while neglecting the crucial task of breaking free from the chains of impiety that ensnared their hearts. In another passage, Isaiah masterfully illustrates the kind of works that ought to flow from true repentance (Isaiah 58:1-14).

Now, let us turn our attention to the second aspect. We have stated that repentance arises from a genuine fear of God. Indeed, before the conscience of a sinner can be led to repentance, it must first be stirred by the weight of God's judgment. When the thought takes hold in the depths of the human heart that one day God will ascend His throne of judgment, demanding an account of all our deeds and words, it becomes an incessant goad, relentlessly urging and compelling the wretched sinner to embrace a new life. This relentless awareness of impending judgment leaves no room for respite or tranquility, but rather, it drives the sinner to continually strive towards a transformed existence, that they may stand securely before the judgment seat. Hence, when scripture exhorts us to repentance, it frequently serves as a reminder that God will one day judge the world. Consider the words of Jeremiah: "lest my wrath go forth like fire, and burn with none to quench it, because of your evil deeds" (Jeremiah 4:4). Similarly, in St. Paul's sermon to the Athenians, he proclaims that God, having permitted people to walk in ignorance, now commands all to repent, for He has appointed a day on which He will judge the world in righteousness (Acts 17:30–31). Numerous other passages echo this sentiment. At times, scripture even underscores the reality of divine judgment through historical events, serving as a sobering reminder to sinners that greater suffering awaits them if they do not mend their ways in due time. We find an example of this in the twenty-ninth chapter of Deuteronomy (Deuteronomy 29:23).

Now, as the commencement of our conversion to God entails a deep-seated abhorrence and dread of sin, the apostle rightly asserts that godly sorrow is the catalyst for repentance. He refers to it as "godly sorrow" (2 Corinthians 7:10), for it is not merely a fear of punishment, but a profound aversion and condemnation of sin itself. This sorrow arises from the understanding that sin is displeasing to God, and thus, we despise and detest it with every fiber of our being.

Let us now delve into the third aspect, wherein we assert that repentance encompasses two fundamental components: the mortification of the flesh and the vivification of the spirit. While the prophets, in their simplicity, conveyed these truths to a people enveloped in ignorance, their teachings aptly expound upon the essence of repentance. They proclaimed, "Cease to do evil and devote yourselves to good," and beckoned, "Cleanse yourselves from your filth, forsake your perverse ways, learn to do good, pursue righteousness and mercy" (Psalm 34:14; Isaiah 1:16-17), and so on. By calling individuals to turn away from malevolence, they demanded nothing less than the crucifixion and demise of the entire sinful nature within them. However, let us not underestimate the arduousness of this commandment, for it necessitates the complete abandonment of self and the annihilation of our very being. To truly put the flesh to death (Romans 8:13), we must renounce everything that is of ourselves and allow it to be reduced to nothingness. You see, every inclination and emotion stemming from our fallen nature stands in opposition to God and acts as an adversary to His righteousness. Therefore, our initial step towards obedience to the law requires the renunciation of our nature and the relinquishment of our own will. Moreover, the prophet's words also signify the renewal of life through subsequent actions, such as righteousness, justice, and mercy. Engaging in external deeds alone would prove insufficient unless our souls first cultivate a genuine love and inclination towards them. This transformation occurs when God's Spirit, in His holiness, remodels our souls, guiding them towards new thoughts and affections, rendering them unrecognizable compared to their former state. Both mortification and vivification find their source in our union with Christ. Indeed, if we are true participants in His death (Romans 6:3ff), the power of His sacrifice crucifies our old selves, putting to death the accumulation of sin within us, and weakening the stronghold of corruption in our original nature. And if we partake in His resurrection, we are resurrected to a new life that aligns with God's righteousness. It is through communion with Christ that these transformative processes unfold within us.

In essence, repentance can be understood as a spiritual rebirth—a process aimed at restoring the divine image within us, an image that was obscured and all but erased through Adam's transgression. The apostle aptly describes this transformation as the removal of the veil from our eyes, allowing us to reflect God's glory and be transformed into His likeness through the work of His Spirit. He urges us to be renewed in our inner selves, to put on the new self created in God's image, characterized by righteousness and true holiness (2 Corinthians 3:18; Ephesians 4:23-24; Colossians 3:10). Through this regeneration, accomplished by the grace of Christ, we are reinstated into God's righteousness, from which we were excluded by the sin of Adam. It pleases God to restore, in their entirety, all those whom He adopts into the inheritance of eternal life, reclaiming them as His own.

Tears and Fasting

Now, let us examine the fruits of repentance. Some individuals, influenced by the passages in which the prophets admonish the people to repent with tears, fasting, and outward signs of mourning— such as wearing sackcloth and ashes on their heads (as notably mentioned in Joel 2:12-13)—erroneously believe that the crux of repentance lies in fasting and weeping. However, we must firmly challenge this misconception. In the passage from Joel, the emphasis is rightly placed on the complete transformation of our hearts, on rending our hearts rather than merely tearing our garments. Tears and fasting are mentioned as circumstantial elements that were particularly fitting for that specific time and context. Joel, having pronounced God's impending judgment upon the people, urges them to avert it not only through a change in their way of life but also by humbling themselves and displaying signs of sorrow. Just as an individual accused of a crime might grow a beard, leave their hair uncombed, and don mourning attire to seek mercy from a judge, so too it was fitting for the people indicted before God's throne to outwardly demonstrate their repentance and plea for pardon, acknowledging that their hope lay solely in His unfathomable mercy.

Although the practices of wearing sackcloth and putting ashes on the head were customary in those days and hold no relevance for us today, we must not dismiss the significance of tears and fasting, particularly when the Lord presents us with signs of impending calamity. When He allows dangers to manifest before us, He signals His readiness to execute judgment, with His divine arm poised for action. Thus, the prophet aptly encourages the shedding of tears and the observance of fasts as visible expressions of genuine sorrow for those whom he had warned of the impending wrath of God. It would be commendable if today's ecclesiastical pastors followed suit. In times when they perceive the approach of calamities, be it war, famine, or plague, they ought to exhort their congregations to turn to the Lord in prayer, accompanied by tears and fasting. However, let us ensure that these acts are rooted in the fundamental task of rending our hearts rather than merely tearing our garments. Undoubtedly, fasting has not always been intrinsically linked to repentance, but it serves as an appropriate means for those who desire to testify that they acknowledge their deserving of God's wrath and yet seek pardon through His boundless mercy. Jesus Christ Himself associates fasting with suffering and affliction. He pardoned His apostles for not fasting during His presence with them, for it was a time of joy. However, He anticipated that they would have the opportunity to fast during moments of sorrow and separation when they would be deprived of His physical company (Matthew 9:15–16). Here, I am referring to solemn and public fasting. Yet, it is crucial to note that the life of a Christian should be characterized by temperance and sobriety, to the extent that it appears to be a perpetual fast, an ongoing state of self-restraint from beginning to end.

Repentance Preached by Christ and His Apostles

Indeed, if we consider the well-established truth that the entire essence of the Gospel revolves around two fundamental pillars, namely, repentance and the forgiveness of sins, we cannot help but recognize that the Lord, in His infinite grace, justifies His servants not only to absolve them of guilt but also to restore them to a state of true righteousness through the sanctifying work of His Spirit. This serves as the very essence of the preaching of John the Baptist, who was divinely appointed as the angelic messenger to pave the way for the coming of Christ. His resounding proclamation echoes through the ages: "Repent, for the kingdom of God is at hand" (Matthew 3:2). By calling the people to repentance, John urges them to acknowledge their sinful condition, to condemn themselves and their works before the Almighty, and to fervently desire the mortification of their flesh and the transformative regeneration of God's Spirit. Simultaneously, his announcement of the kingdom of God is an invitation to faith. When he declares that the kingdom of God is near, he is signifying the arrival of forgiveness of sins, salvation, life, and all the blessings bestowed upon us through Christ. It is for this reason that the other evangelists testify, "John appeared, baptizing in the wilderness and proclaiming a baptism of repentance for the forgiveness of sins" (Mark 1:4; Luke 3:3). This indicates that he preached to people who were burdened by the weight of their transgressions, directing them back to God and instilling within them

the hope of His abundant grace and salvation.

In a similar manner, Christ initiated His sermons by declaring, "The kingdom of God is near; repent and believe in the gospel." Firstly, He proclaims the opening of the divine storehouses of mercy in Himself; secondly, He calls for genuine repentance; and finally, He emphasizes unwavering confidence in God's promises. In another passage, seeking to encapsulate the entirety of the gospel message, He states that it was imperative for Him to suffer, be raised from the dead, and for repentance and the forgiveness of sins to be proclaimed in His name (Luke 24:46–47). The apostles echoed this proclamation after His resurrection, testifying that God had raised Him up to grant repentance and forgiveness of sins to the people of Israel (Acts 5:30– 31). Penitence is preached in the name of Christ when the teachings of the Gospel expose the corruption that permeates human thoughts, affections, and actions, prompting the recognition that regeneration is necessary for anyone seeking entry into the kingdom of God. Forgiveness of sins is preached when individuals are shown that Christ is their redemption, righteousness, salvation, and life, and through Him, they are accounted as righteous and blameless before God. Consequently, His righteousness is freely credited to them. Both repentance and the remission of sins are received through faith. However, since the focal point of faith is the goodness of God, by which our sins are pardoned, it becomes necessary to differentiate between faith and repentance.

Repentance and Change of Life

The initial step in repentance, which stems from a genuine abhorrence for sin, grants us the first glimpse into the knowledge of Christ. It is in the hearts of impoverished and afflicted sinners, those who groan under the weight of their transgressions, who labor tirelessly, burdened and famished, overwhelmed by their afflictions and wretchedness, that Christ chooses to reveal Himself (Isaiah 61:1; Matthew 11:4–5). Conversely, once we embark on the path of repentance, it is a lifelong journey that should persist until our final breath if we desire to find true rest and abide in Christ. He came to summon sinners, but His call is an invitation to repentance (Matthew 9:13; Acts 5:31). Though He blesses the unworthy, it is with the expectation that each individual turns away from their sinful ways. This sentiment is echoed throughout Scripture. Therefore, when the Lord bestows upon us the remission of sins, it is customary for Him to request a corresponding amendment of life, emphasizing that His mercy ought to serve as the impetus and foundation for our transformation. He declares, "Execute justice and righteousness, for salvation is near." Furthermore, He proclaims, "Salvation will come to Zion, to those in Israel who turn from their transgressions." And He exhorts, "Seek the Lord while He may be found; call upon Him while He is near. Let the wicked forsake his way, and the unrighteous man his thoughts; let him return to the Lord, that He may have compassion on him" (Isaiah 56:1, 59:20, 55:6–7). Likewise, the apostle urges, "Repent therefore and turn back, that your sins may be blotted out" (Acts 3:19). However, we must note in this passage that the condition is not presented as the foundation for obtaining pardon. On the contrary, since the Lord desires to extend mercy to humanity for the purpose of facilitating their amendment of life, we are reminded of the ultimate goal we must strive for if we seek to receive forgiveness from God.

In the confines of our mortal bodies, we find ourselves engaged in an unceasing struggle against the corruption that permeates our very nature. Plato, in his musings, proclaimed that the life of a philosopher is a meditation on death. Yet, we can assert with greater veracity that the life of a Christian is characterized by a relentless endeavor and unyielding discipline in mortifying the flesh. It is through the death of our sinful nature that the Spirit of God may truly reign within us. Thus, I believe that those who have acquired a profound discontentment with themselves have made significant progress. However, let us not remain stagnant at this point, but rather, let us direct our aspirations and yearnings towards God. Through our grafting into the death and resurrection of Christ, let us persevere in a continuous state of repentance.

Indeed, those who are genuinely moved by a detestation of sin cannot do otherwise, for one does not develop a hatred for sin without first being captivated by a love for righteousness. This simple truth resonates deeply with the teachings of Scripture, as it reflects the profound interplay between sin and righteousness.

Repentance Not Understood by the Scholastics

Now, let us turn our attention to the perspectives espoused by the sophists regarding repentance. I shall endeavor to address their teachings concisely, as brevity is my aim in this writing. Delving too deeply into their convoluted arguments would only lead us further into their intricate mazes, making it arduous to find an escape from their clutches. Therefore, let us tread cautiously, mindful of the potential complexities that lie ahead, while seeking clarity and understanding in this matter.

It appears that those who claim to provide a definition of repentance have utterly failed to grasp its true essence. Their reliance on select quotations from the early church fathers, though seemingly profound, falls short of capturing the profound nature and essence of repentance. Let us examine these statements they present:

"To do repentance is to weep for sins previously committed and not to commit those for which they must afterward weep." And, "It is to groan for all past evils and no longer commit those for which they must afterward groan." These utterances, while appealing on the surface, fail to encompass the depth and significance of repentance. They serve merely as exhortations to penitents, urging them to refrain from falling into the same sins from which they have been delivered.

It is worth noting that, even if one were inclined to regard these statements as accurate definitions, it would be just as easy for a contentious individual to refute them. After all, should we accept everything uttered by the early church fathers as definitive statements, there exist other quotations of seemingly equal value. For instance, St. Chrysostom described repentance as a curative medicine, a divine gift bestowed from above, an astonishing power transcending earthly laws.

However, let us not be swayed by these isolated proclamations. It is crucial to discern the true meaning of repentance, one that transcends mere exhortations and quotations. Only then can we attain a comprehensive understanding of this transformative spiritual discipline.

Having presented their subtle definition of repentance, these scholars proceed to divide it into three parts: contrition of heart, confession of mouth, and satisfaction of works. They seem to take great delight in their ability to divide and define, honed as they are in the art of dialectic. However, their division is as ill-fitting as their definition, despite their lifelong devotion to the study of such matters.

If one were to challenge them, employing their own definition as an argument, suggesting that a person can weep for past sins and abstain from committing them again without confessing with the mouth, how would they defend their division? If it is indeed true that a person who does not confess orally can still be a genuine penitent, then repentance can exist without this particular aspect of confession. If they respond by asserting that this division should pertain to repentance as a sacrament or to its complete perfection, which they fail to grasp in their definitions, then they have no reason to criticize me. Rather, the fault lies with their lack of clarity and purity in their definitions.

It is vital to recognize that the matter at hand is not a trivial dispute, but a question of immense significance—the forgiveness of sins. When these scholars insist on these three elements—heartfelt regret, verbal confession, and works of satisfaction—as necessary for repentance, it implies that these requirements are essential for obtaining forgiveness. If there is anything we must truly comprehend in our religious understanding, it is this: the means, the manner, the conditions, and the level of difficulty or ease involved in obtaining the remission of sins. Without certainty and clarity in this knowledge, the conscience remains restless and at odds, lacking peace with God, confidence, and assurance. It is in a constant state of trembling, turmoil, torment, and dread of God's judgment, striving to flee from it whenever possible. If the forgiveness of sins is contingent upon the conditions they impose, then we are left in a state of wretchedness and despair unlike any other.

The Doctrine of Contrition as Taught by the Scholatics

The theologians, in their wisdom, prescribe contrition as the first essential step towards obtaining pardon and grace. They insist that this contrition must be done properly, fully, and entirely. Yet, they fail to provide any clear guidelines as to when one can be certain that they have truly accomplished this contrition and fulfilled their obligation. Poor consciences are left in a state of tremendous distress and anguish, for they are burdened with the requirement of due contrition without knowing the magnitude of the debt, unable to ascertain when they have paid what is owed.

If theologians assert that we must do what lies within our power, we find ourselves trapped in an endless cycle. When can one ever dare to assure themselves that they have exerted all their strength in weeping for their sins? Consequently, after much internal debate, consciences, desperate for relief and unable to find solace or refuge, may resort to self-imposed affliction and forcibly extract tears, all in the name of fulfilling this contrition. If theologians wish to accuse me of slander, I challenge them to present a single person who has not been plunged into despair by such teachings, or a solitary individual who has not feigned affliction as a feeble attempt to appease God's judgment, while true remorse remains elusive.

In the face of such a predicament, it is crucial to reflect upon the implications of this theological position. How can consciences find genuine peace and reassurance when the standard for contrition remains undefined and unattainable? Is it not time to reconsider and seek a more merciful and gracious approach that aligns with the compassionate nature of our loving Creator? Let us earnestly explore the depths of divine forgiveness and the boundless nature of God's grace, for it is in embracing the magnitude of His mercy that true contrition and transformation can be found.

We have previously stated that forgiveness of sins is never granted without repentance, for it is through genuine and heartfelt affliction and wounded conscience that one can sincerely implore God's mercy. However, let us be clear that repentance itself is not the cause of this forgiveness, thereby relieving souls from the torment of feeling obligated to perfectly accomplish contrition. Instead, we instruct the sinner to shift their gaze from their own regret and tears and fix their eyes upon the boundless mercy of God.

Moreover, we emphasize that it is those who labor and carry burdens who are called by Christ. He was sent to proclaim good news to the impoverished, to heal the wounded hearts, to offer liberation to the captives, freedom to the prisoners, and solace to those in mourning (Matthew 11:5; Isaiah 61:1). This excludes the Pharisees who were self-righteous and blind to their own poverty, as well as those who scorn God, showing no concern for His wrath and seeking no remedy for their wickedness. Such individuals do not labor, they are not afflicted in their hearts, nor are they bound or captive; they do not weep. There exists a profound distinction between instructing a sinner to strive for forgiveness by achieving full and complete contrition, an impossible task as propagated by these theologians, and guiding them to hunger and thirst for God's mercy through a recognition of their own wretchedness. We exhort them to embrace their toil, affliction, and captivity, leading them to seek comfort, rest, and deliverance. In essence, we teach them to glorify God through humility.

Confession: A So-Called Proof From Scripture

Regarding the matter of confession, an age-old controversy has persisted between the canonists and scholastic theologians. The former assert that confession is merely a product of human legislation, an ordinance established by ecclesiastical authorities. On the other hand, the latter claim that confession is divinely commanded. This ongoing dispute serves as a stark reminder of the audacity displayed by theologians, who, in their pursuit, have manipulated and distorted numerous passages of scripture to support their own agenda. Yet, recognizing the futility of their efforts, the most cunning among them have devised a clever escape route, suggesting that confession possesses divine origins in its essence but has adopted its specific form through human law. Such reasoning mirrors the feeble attempts of those less versed in legal matters who twist the words directed at Adam—"Adam, where are you?"—to substantiate divine law. Similarly, they attribute divine law to the subsequent response wherein Adam, in his defense, implicates the woman given to him by God. However, it is worth noting that the formulation of confession, both shaped and unshaped, owes its existence to civil law, not divine law!

Now, let us examine the arguments put forth by these theologians in an attempt to prove that God commanded confession, whether in its current form or otherwise. They argue, "Our Lord sent the lepers to the priests" (Matthew 8:4; Luke 5:14, 17:14). But why did He send them? Was it to confess their sins? Has it ever been heard that the Levitical priests were ordained to hear confessions (Deuteronomy 17:8-9)? This prompts these theologians to resort to allegory, asserting, "The Mosaic law dictated that priests should distinguish between different types of leprosy, and sin is spiritual leprosy, thus falling under the purview of the priest's judgment." Before addressing this, I pose a question: If, according to this passage, priests were appointed as judges of spiritual leprosy, why do they also claim authority over the recognition of natural and bodily leprosy? Is it not a blatant manipulation of scripture to alter its meaning in such a manner?

"The law assigns the judgment of leprosy to the Levitical priests; let us then appropriate it for ourselves. Sin is spiritual leprosy; therefore, let us assume the role of sin's judges."

I must emphasize that since the priesthood has been transferred, it is imperative that the law be transferred as well. With Jesus Christ as the fulfillment and culmination of all priesthoods, He assumes all the dignity and prerogative associated with it. If these theologians find delight in allegories, let them present Christ as the sole Priest and bestow upon Him all jurisdiction; we can easily embrace this proposition. However, the allegory they employ is misguided, as it conflates purely civil law with ceremonial practices. So, why does Christ send the lepers to the priests? It is to prevent the priests from accusing Him of transgressing the law, which stipulates that the one healed of leprosy should present themselves before the priest and undergo purification through a prescribed offering. He commands the lepers whom He had healed to fulfill the requirements of the law, saying, "Go, show yourselves to the priests and offer the gift that Moses commanded, as a testimony to them" (Matthew 8:4; Mark 1:44; Luke 5:14). Indeed, this miracle should serve as a testimony to them. The priests had declared these individuals as lepers, and now they must acknowledge their healing. Are they not, against their own will, compelled to bear witness to the miracles of Christ? He allows them to test the authenticity of His miracle, leaving them with no option but to acknowledge it. Yet, despite these undeniable proofs, they persist in their equivocation. Thus, this miraculous work stands as a witness against them. As another passage states, "And this gospel of the kingdom will be proclaimed throughout the whole world as a testimony to all nations" (Matthew 24:14). Additionally, it is said, "You will be brought before kings and governors for my name's sake. This will be your opportunity to bear witness to them" (Matthew 10:18), signifying that they will be further convicted at the divine judgment. If these theologians prefer to rely on the authority of St. Chrysostom, let it be known that he teaches that Christ acted in this manner because of the Jews, so as not to be seen as one who disregarded the law.

Confession: A Second So-Called Proof From Scripture

These theologians, ever fond of their allegories, present their second argument from the same source as if allegories possess some great power to substantiate their teachings! Yet, I would be content if allegories alone were sufficient, especially since I could claim them with greater legitimacy than they can. They claim that after Jesus raised Lazarus from the dead, He commanded His disciples to unbind and free him (John 11:44). Firstly, they blatantly deceive with their assertion, for nowhere does it state that He commanded His disciples to perform such a task. It is far more plausible that He directed those words to the Jews present at the scene, so that the miracle would be evident without a shadow of doubt, eliminating any suspicion of trickery. His power would appear even more remarkable as He raised the dead through the sheer force of His word, without physical contact. Indeed, I understand it in this manner: our Lord, seeking to remove any wicked doubt from the minds of the Jews, desired them to roll away the stone, perceive the putrid stench, witness the unmistakable signs of death, and then behold Lazarus resurrected solely by the power of His commanding voice. They would be the first to touch Lazarus, serving as living testimony to the miracle. Nevertheless, let us hypothetically grant that these words were spoken to the disciples. What, then, do these theologians deduce from this? How can they further expound upon this passage through their cherished allegory? Perhaps they will suggest that our Lord intended to teach His faithful to release those whom He had resurrected. That is to say, they should not recall the sins that He has forgotten, nor condemn those whom He has absolved. They should not make accusations about matters for which He has granted pardon, nor be harsh and unyielding in punishment when He, in His mercy, has been gracious, tender, and compassionate in extending forgiveness! Oh, let these theologians behold the brilliance of their allegories and wield them as their shield and authority!

Confession: Two New Testament Texts Explored

They make an attempt to bolster their position by citing supposedly clear passages from Scripture. They argue, "Those who came to John's baptism confessed their sins, and James commands us to confess our sins to one another" (Matthew 3:6; James 5:16). To this, I respond that it is no revelation that those who sought baptism from John confessed their sins. After all, John had been preaching a baptism of repentance and administered water baptism for the purpose of repentance. Whom else would he baptize except those who openly acknowledged themselves as sinners? Baptism serves as a symbol of forgiveness of sins; naturally, it is reserved for sinners who recognize their need for such forgiveness. Hence, they confessed their sins in order to partake in baptism. There is indeed good reason for James to instruct us to confess to one another. However, if these theologians paid closer attention to what follows, they would discover that it hardly supports their argument. James continues, "Confess your sins to one another and pray for one another" (James 5:16). He intertwines mutual prayer and mutual confession. If it were necessary to confess solely to priests, then it would logically follow that we should pray exclusively for them as well. According to James' words, only priests would have the privilege of confessing. After all, if he instructs us to confess to one another mutually or reciprocally, it implies that the confessor must also hear the confession of the other person. This privilege, however, they reserve exclusively for priests. Therefore, in accordance with their own line of reasoning, we shall willingly concede to them the duty of confessing!

Let us discard such nonsensical arguments and grasp the straightforward and clear meaning of the apostle. He teaches us to communicate and reveal our weaknesses to one another, seeking counsel, compassion, and mutual comfort. Moreover, let us be aware of the weaknesses of our brothers and sisters, and let each one of us, in turn, pray to God for these very weaknesses. So why do they wield St. James against us? We ardently emphasize the need for confessing our unworthiness before God, for it is through this confession that we can humbly acknowledge His boundless mercy. We go even further and declare that all who fail to confess their sins before God, His angels, the church, and indeed, all people, are cursed and condemned. For God has encompassed all under the weight of sin, so that every mouth may be silenced, every human being humbled, and He alone may be justified and exalted. (Galatians 3:22; Romans 3:9, 19).

Confession in Church History

I find it truly astonishing how audacious they are to assert that the confession they speak of is rooted in divine law. While we acknowledge that the practice of confession is ancient, we can easily demonstrate that it was initially voluntary. Their own histories attest to the fact that there was no law or decree until the time of Innocent

III. Numerous accounts from ancient writers and historians reveal that it was a disciplinary measure instituted solely by the bishops, rather than an ordinance established by Christ or His apostles. Allow me to present just one of these historical records, which should suffice to support my argument.

Sozomen, a respected author of Ecclesiastical History, recounts that this practice was a decree specifically observed in the western churches, particularly at Rome. This clearly indicates that it was not a universal practice throughout all the churches. Furthermore, Sozomen highlights the fact that a designated priest was assigned to this role, thereby debunking the theologians' claim that the keys were indiscriminately bestowed upon the entire priestly order. It was not a responsibility shared by all, but rather the duty of a chosen individual elected by the bishop for this purpose.

Moreover, Sozomen mentions that this practice was followed in Constantinople until an incident occurred involving a woman who deceitfully used confession as a pretext to engage in an inappropriate relationship with one of the deacons. As a result of this immoral behavior, Nectarius, the esteemed bishop of Constantinople known for his holiness and profound teaching, abolished the practice of confession. I suggest these individuals lend their ears to this historical account and reconsider their stance.

Let us reflect deeply on the origins and development of confession, seeking wisdom and discernment in our understanding. May we always turn to the true source of authority, the teachings of Christ and His apostles, guided by the light of reason and the guidance of the Holy Spirit.

If auricular confession were truly a divine law, how could Nectarius have had the audacity to abolish it? Are these theologians accusing this revered and esteemed figure, who was respected by all the early church fathers, of heresy and schism? By their own reasoning, they would condemn not only Nectarius but also the entire church of Constantinople, as well as all the eastern churches, for supposedly disregarding an inviolable law imposed upon all Christians. It is truly astounding that they dare to open their mouths and speak against the actions of these individuals.

The fact is that the abolition of confession is abundantly supported by the teachings of St. Chrysostom, who himself served as the bishop of Constantinople. His words are so clear and explicit on this matter that it is astonishing these theologians have the audacity to challenge them. He unequivocally states, "If you want to wipe out sins, confess them. If you are ashamed to disclose them to a person, confess them every day in your soul. Confess them to God, who can purify them. Confess them on your bed, in order that your conscience may each day recognize its evil." Furthermore, he emphasizes, "It is not necessary to confess before a witness; only make the acknowledgment in your heart; this examination does not require a witness; it is enough that God alone may see and hear you." St. Chrysostom repeatedly stresses that there is no need to confess to a person who may later rebuke or shame you, but rather one should bring their wounds before God, the compassionate Healer of souls.

Shall we then claim that St. Chrysostom, in speaking in such a manner, was so reckless as to release people's consciences from the very bonds that God had ordained? Certainly not. What he understood as not being commanded by God, he did not dare to impose as necessary. He recognized the true healing power that comes from confessing our sins to God alone, without the need for a human intermediary. St. Chrysostom understood that it is in God's presence, in the depths of our hearts, where true repentance and healing occur.

Confession of Sins According to Holy Writ

Let us therefore ponder the wisdom of these teachings, and let us approach confession with a sincere and contrite heart, seeking reconciliation with God and allowing His grace to transform us. May we never impose unnecessary burdens on ourselves or others, but instead embrace the freedom and mercy offered to us through Christ.

To delve into this matter further, let us faithfully expound on the nature of confession as revealed in God's Word. We shall then address their fabrications regarding confession, albeit not exhaustively (for who could drain such a vast sea?), but focusing on the crux of their teachings. It is worth noting that scripture often employs the term "confession" in the context of praise, a fact that these audacious individuals conveniently ignore as they wield such passages to bolster their claims. Take, for instance, their assertion that confession engenders joy in the heart, citing the Psalm: "With the voice of joy and confession" (Psalm 42:4). May the uninformed grasp the true meaning of these words and learn to discern it from the other, so as not to fall easily into the trap of such falsehoods.

Regarding the confession of sins, scripture instructs us as follows: since it is the Lord who forgives, forgets, and blots out our transgressions, let us confess them before Him to obtain grace and pardon. He is the Divine Physician, so let us present to Him our wounds and sores. It is He who has been offended and wounded, so let us implore His mercy and seek reconciliation. He knows the depths of our hearts and sees every thought, therefore, let us lay open our hearts before Him. It is He who calls sinners, so let us turn to Him in repentance. As David proclaims, "I acknowledged my sin to you, and I did not cover my iniquity; I said, 'I will confess my transgressions to the Lord,' and you forgave the iniquity of my sin" (Psalm 32:5). David's plea for mercy echoes the same sentiment: "Have mercy on me, O Lord, according to your steadfast love" (Psalm 51:1). Daniel also offers a similar confession: "We have sinned and done wrong and acted wickedly and rebelled, turning aside from your commandments" (Daniel 9:5). Scripture abounds with comparable examples.

Indeed, as St. John affirms, "If we confess our sins, he is faithful and just to forgive us our sins" (1 John 1:9). It is through confession, directed toward our merciful Lord, that we find solace in the assurance of His forgiveness. The act of confessing our sins is a means by which we acknowledge our brokenness before God and seek His loving restoration. So let us approach Him with contrite hearts, knowing that He is faithful and compassionate, ready to embrace us and grant us reconciliation. May this understanding of confession guide us on our journey of faith, leading us to a deeper relationship with our forgiving God.

To whom do we confess our sins? Surely, it is to Him—the Almighty. But on one condition: with a contrite and humble heart, we prostrate ourselves before Him, honestly acknowledging our faults and seeking absolution through His infinite goodness and mercy. Whoever truly confesses before God will surely find their tongue ready to proclaim His mercy among the people. It is not merely a whisper in secrecy, but a courageous disclosure of our poverty and a testament to God's glory, not just once, but repeatedly, openly, and for all to hear.

Consider the example of David, who, after being confronted by Nathan and pierced by the prick of conscience, confessed his sin both to God and before the people. He declared, "I have sinned against the Lord" (2 Samuel 12:13). No more excuses or equivocations. He desired that his guilt be evident, not only to God but also to his fellow human beings. Let us follow this solemn confession, akin to the collective repentance of Nehemiah and Ezra's time (Ezra 10:1–17; Nehemiah 9:1–37). All churches should emulate this practice when seeking God's forgiveness, as it is customary among well-ordered congregations.

Furthermore, the Scriptures commend to us two additional forms of confession. The first is for our own benefit. It is what St. James speaks of when he urges us to confess our sins to one another (James 5:16). The intention behind this is that by revealing our weaknesses to each other, we may mutually offer counsel and comfort. The second form of confession is driven by love for our neighbor, who has been wounded by our transgressions. It aims to reconcile and restore peace with them. Christ Himself addresses this in the Gospel of Matthew, saying, "If you are offering your gift at the altar and there remember that your brother has something against you, leave your gift there before the altar and go. First be reconciled to your brother, and then come and offer your gift" (Matthew 5:23-24). Through confessing our sins, we seek to mend the bonds of love that have been strained by our offenses.

As for the first form of confession, though Scripture does not designate a specific person to whom we must unload our burdens, it allows us the freedom to choose a trustworthy fellow believer who can lend a listening ear to our confession. However, it is worth noting that pastors are particularly suited for this role. Their divine appointment as shepherds of God's flock positions them to guide us in overcoming sin and to proclaim God's goodness for our comfort. Thus, when one finds their conscience entangled in such perplexity that they cannot find solace alone, it is wise not to disregard the remedy graciously offered by God. Let them, with prudence, confess individually to their pastor and receive the solace and comfort that comes from the pastor's ministry. After all, it is the pastor's responsibility to bring solace to God's people through the individual teaching of the gospel, as well as in public gatherings. However, let us

always maintain the balance that conscience must not be ensnared and subjected to a yoke in matters where God has granted us freedom.

Roman Catholicism's False Doctrine on the Power of the Keys

In examining the pages of Scripture, we find no trace of the confessional practice concocted by those theologians. Oh no, they have devised a grand scheme of their own! According to their decree, all individuals, regardless of gender, once they reach the age of discretion, are obligated to confess each and every sin to their own parish priest at least once a year. As for the remission of sins, it is contingent upon one's unwavering intention to confess. Should that intention be unfulfilled when the opportunity arises, any hopes of entering paradise are dashed. Furthermore, the priest holds the vaunted power of the keys—the authority to bind or loose the sinner. They vehemently argue that the words of Christ, that which they bind on earth shall be bound in heaven (Matthew 16:19; cf. Matthew 18:18), cannot be rendered meaningless.

Ah, but here's where the contention arises among their ranks. Some claim that there is essentially only one key—the power to bind and loose—and that while knowledge is required to wield it correctly, it is merely an ancillary component and not its essence. Others, noticing the sheer disorderliness of such a notion, have devised a division of keys: discretion and power. And yet others, seeking to temper the caprice of the priests, have introduced additional keys: the authority to distinguish (employed when issuing definitive verdicts) and power (employed when enforcing said verdicts). They have even appended knowledge as a counselor. Alas, they dare not simply interpret binding and loosing as the forgiveness and absolution of sins, for they hear the Lord Himself declare through His prophet, "I, I am he who blots out your transgressions for my own sake" (Isaiah 43:25). Instead, they assert that it is the prerogative of the priest to pronounce who is bound and who is loosed, to declare which sins are retained and which are forgiven. They claim that the priest makes these proclamations during the act of confession, when he absolves or retains sins, or through his verdict when he excommunicates or absolves from excommunication.

Nevertheless, they cannot escape the undeniable fact that the unworthy are often bound or loosed by their priests, despite their lack of heavenly authority for such actions. As their last line of defense, they contend that the bestowal of the keys must come with certain limitations. They argue that Christ promised that when a priest's verdict is justly pronounced in accordance with the merits of the individual being bound or loosed, it will be ratified in heaven. Furthermore, they claim that these keys were granted to all priests and are conferred upon them by bishops during their ordination from deacon to priest. However, the exercise of this power is restricted to those in ecclesiastical office. Thus, the keys always remain with priests, even when excommunicated or suspended, albeit rusted and rendered impotent.

Those who assert such claims may appear somewhat reasonable when compared to others who have forged new keys, as if fashioning their own custom locks, to guard what they call the "treasure of the church." They audaciously label the merits of Jesus Christ, the apostles, martyrs, and other saints as this so-called treasure. They contend that the supreme guardianship of this vault has been entrusted to the Bishop of Rome, who holds the key to the initial distribution of these spiritual goods. He, in turn, can bestow them upon others and delegate the authority to distribute them further. And thus, indulgences were born—sometimes granted by the Pope as a plenary remission, at times for a specific number of years, while cardinals received a hundred days and bishops a mere forty.

Obligatory Confession a Cruel Affliction of Conscience

I shall address each of these points briefly, but for now, let us set aside the discussion of the rights and insults they hurl upon the souls of the faithful, for that shall be examined in due course. As for their imposition of a law that necessitates the enumeration of all sins and their denial of forgiveness unless one possesses an unwavering intention to confess, while also proclaiming that the gates of paradise are shut tight against those who spurn the opportunity to confess— such notions are utterly intolerable. How do they expect one to compile a comprehensive list of sins? Even David, who undoubtedly pondered deeply upon the confession of his own transgressions, could not do more than exclaim, "Who can discern his errors? Declare me innocent from hidden faults!" (Psalm 19:12). In another place, he laments, "My iniquities have gone over my head;

like a heavy burden, they are too heavy for me" (Psalm 38:4). Indeed, he understood the profound depths of our sins, the multitude of offenses dwelling within each person, the many heads of this monstrous entity called sin, and the lengthy tail it drags behind. David did not endeavor to provide a complete reckoning but, from the depths of his sinfulness, he cried out to God, saying, "I am submerged, buried, suffocated; the gates of hell have enclosed around me. Let your right hand rescue me from this pit of drowning, from this abyss of death into which I have fallen!" Who now, in light of David's struggle to fathom the number of his own sins, would dare to believe they can meticulously account for their own?

The torments inflicted upon the consciences of those who had a glimpse of God's presence resembled the fires of Gehenna. They embarked on an arduous task of accounting, meticulously dissecting sins into arms, branches, and leaves, following the classifications of these self-proclaimed experts of confession. They meticulously weighed the characteristics, quantities, and circumstances of each transgression. At the outset, they may have made some progress, but as they delved deeper, all they could see was an endless expanse of sky and sea, devoid of any safe harbor or resting place. The further they ventured, the more the numbers multiplied, rising before their eyes like towering mountains that obstructed their view, leaving no hope of ever escaping this labyrinthine maze. Thus, they remained trapped in this anguish, finding no resolution but sinking deeper into despair.

Then, like inhumane executioners, theologians presented a remedy for the wounds and sores they had inflicted upon these tortured souls. Their solution? Each individual should do what was within their power. Yet, new worries pierced them, and fresh torments flayed these hapless beings as thoughts haunted their minds: "I haven't devoted enough time to it. I haven't zealously pursued it as I should have. I've neglected certain aspects due to my own carelessness and inexcusable negligence." The theologians, in their attempt to soften these afflictions, added other prescriptions: "Do penance for your negligence! If it isn't too grave, you may find forgiveness."

But these measures fail to heal the wounds; they are more akin to poisons coated with honey, designed to mask their bitterness and deceive before their true nature is revealed. This dreadful voice incessantly echoes in their ears: "Confess all your sins." The horror it invokes cannot be pacified except by a certain and unwavering comfort. The fact that a significant portion of the world has fallen prey to such seductive notions, wherein a lethal poison is disguised as sweetness, does not stem from their belief that God is appeased or that they find contentment within themselves. Rather, it is akin to sailors dropping anchor in the middle of the sea, seeking respite from the toils of their voyage, or a weary pilgrim who, exhausted and stumbling, sits by the wayside to rest. They have sought this temporary reprieve, though it proves woefully insufficient for their true needs.

I will not labor extensively to prove what is evident to each individual's experience. However, let me succinctly describe the nature of this law. Firstly, it is utterly impossible, inevitably leading to ruin, damnation, confusion, and the utter destruction of those who adhere to it, plunging them into despair. Moreover, by diverting sinners from a genuine understanding of their transgressions, it transforms them into hypocrites who remain ignorant of both God and themselves. By obsessing over the enumeration of their sins, they conveniently forget the hidden abyss of vice residing deep within their hearts—their concealed iniquities and impurities. To truly apprehend such darkness, one must primarily contemplate their own wretchedness. In contrast, the proper manner of confession lies in acknowledging and confessing an abyss of evil within us, one that overwhelms our senses. We witness this form of confession in the words of the publican: "Lord, be merciful to me, a sinner," implying, "All that exists within me is but sin, so immense that neither my thoughts nor my tongue can fully grasp its magnitude. May the abyss of Your mercy swallow up the abyss of my sins!"

"But," someone might inquire, "is it not necessary to confess each sin? Does God not find satisfaction in confession unless it is expressed in these few words: 'I am a sinner'?" I respond that our utmost endeavor should be to lay bare our entire heart before God, as far as humanly possible. It is not merely a matter of confessing our status as sinners but genuinely embracing that identity, recognizing, with utmost contemplation, the vast extent and various forms of our sinful filth. We must acknowledge not only our impurity but also the specific nature of our impurity, contemplating its enormity and multiplicity. We must acknowledge not only our indebtedness but also the overwhelming burden of debts that weigh us down. We must acknowledge not only our wounds but the multitude, gravity, and mortal nature of these wounds. Nevertheless, even when a sinner has bared their soul before God with such awareness, they must sincerely believe that numerous other evils still reside within them, which they cannot fully comprehend. The depth of their wretchedness is such that minutely examining it or discovering its boundaries becomes an arduous task. Hence, let them cry out, echoing the words of David: "Who can discern their own errors? Cleanse me from hidden faults!" (Psalm 19:12).

Furthermore, these theologians have the audacity to claim that sins are not forgiven unless one possesses a specific intention to confess, and that the gates of paradise remain firmly shut to those who pass up the opportunity for confession. How absurd it is for us to concur with such notions! The forgiveness of sins has not changed; it remains consistent throughout history. We find no mention of those who obtained forgiveness of sins from Christ being required to whisper their confessions into the ear of a certain Mr. John. How could they confess when confessors did not yet exist, and the practice of confession itself was unknown for a considerable time? Yet, even during that period of ignorance, sins were forgiven without the conditions these theologians impose. Let us not dispute this matter as if it were a dubious proposition, for the eternal Word of God is unambiguous: "When the wicked person turns away from his wickedness, he shall save his life. He shall live" (Ezekiel 18:27). Those who dare to add conditions to this divine promise do not bind sins but rather restrict God's boundless mercy.

Auricular Confession a Plague

It comes as no surprise, then, that we reject this auricular confession, a plague-like and perilous phenomenon that poses numerous threats to the Church. Even if it were a matter of indifference, its lack of fruitfulness and utility, coupled with the multitude of errors, sacrileges, and impieties it has spawned, make it worthy of abolition. Certainly, these theologians boast about certain advantages that they claim arise from auricular confession, extolling them to the utmost. However, these so-called benefits are either fabricated or trivial. They particularly emphasize the value of shame experienced by the penitent, arguing that it serves as a severe affliction that leads to greater vigilance in the future and prevents God's vengeance by inflicting self-punishment. But are we not subjecting individuals to immense shame when we summon them to this lofty heavenly tribunal and to the judgment of God? Is it truly a great gain if we refrain from sinning due to our embarrassment before others, yet harbor no shame in the presence of God, who bears witness to our wicked conscience? Such a notion is utterly false and misguided.

Let us not be deceived by these fallacies and illusions. Let us instead turn our hearts and minds toward genuine repentance, seeking the boundless mercy and forgiveness of our gracious Lord. It is in sincere contrition and humble submission to God that we find true reconciliation and renewal.

Behold the remarkable phenomenon that ensues after people have made their confessions to the priest! It appears that they acquire an unparalleled boldness and license to commit evil, as if they could simply wipe their mouths clean and proclaim that all scores against them have been erased. Not only does this embolden them to sin throughout the entire year, but it also relieves them of any concern about confession for the remaining months. They cease to sigh for God, neglecting introspection, and instead accumulate sin upon sin until, in their minds, they disgorge all their transgressions together once again when the next confession period arrives. And once they have regurgitated their sins, they believe they have effectively discharged their burdens and evaded God's judgment, which they have conveniently transferred to the priest. They delude themselves into thinking that God will forget what they have revealed to the priest.

Furthermore, who among them approaches the day of confession with a sense of courage and readiness? Who goes to confession with a truly sincere heart, rather than being dragged there like a reluctant prisoner, compelled against their will? (Except, perhaps, the priests themselves, who delight in joyously recounting their own deeds to one another as if they were pleasant tales.) I shall not waste much ink recounting the repugnant abominations that pervade auricular confession. I shall only say this: if the venerable Nectarius, that holy man we mentioned earlier, had not acted wisely in removing confession from his church or indeed eradicating it altogether, merely in response to a single rumor of fornication, then we are sufficiently forewarned today to take similar action in the face of the countless debaucheries, fornications, adulteries, and incestuous acts that are bred from this practice.

The Power of the Keys

Let us now delve into the power of the keys, the very foundation on which these self-proclaimed "confessionists" base their authority.

They raise the question, "Were the keys given without reason? Would Christ have spoken in vain when He declared, 'Whatever you bind on earth will be bound in heaven'?" To this, I respond that there is indeed a profound reason behind the giving of the keys. However, we must be careful to distinguish between the two passages where the Lord testifies that the binding and loosing on earth corresponds to binding and loosing in heaven. It is a lamentable ignorance that leads these wild boars, in their usual manner, to confuse these passages and muddle their meanings.

One of these passages is found in the Gospel of John, where Christ, in commissioning His apostles to preach, breathes upon them and imparts these words: "Receive the Holy Spirit. If you forgive anyone's sins, they are forgiven; if you retain anyone's sins, they are retained." Here, the keys of the kingdom of heaven, previously promised to St. Peter, are bestowed upon him and his fellow apostles. Nothing was promised to Peter alone that he did not equally receive along with the others. It was said to him, "I will give you the keys of the kingdom of heaven." In this instance, all the apostles are instructed to proclaim the gospel, which opens the door of the heavenly kingdom to those who seek the Father through Christ, while closing and barring it to those who turn away from this path. It was said to Peter, "Whatever you bind on earth will be bound in heaven, and whatever you loose on earth will be loosed in heaven." Similarly, it is now declared to all of them collectively, "If you forgive anyone's sins, they are forgiven; if you retain anyone's sins, they are retained." Binding, therefore, signifies the retention of sins, while loosing signifies the pardoning of sins. Indeed, through the remission of sins, consciences are freed from their true chains, whereas the retention of sins keeps them tightly bound. Allow me to offer an interpretation of this passage that is straightforward, genuine, and appropriate, avoiding excessive subtleties or strained explanations.

The commandment to forgive or retain sins, as well as the promise given to St. Peter regarding binding and loosing, should be understood in connection with the ministry of the Word. When our Lord established this ministry for His apostles, He entrusted to them the authority to bind and loose. After all, what is the essence of the gospel if not the proclamation that all of us, enslaved by sin and death, can find deliverance and redemption through Jesus Christ? Conversely, those who fail to recognize and embrace Christ as their Liberator and Redeemer are condemned to eternal imprisonment.

By entrusting this sacred mission to His apostles, our Lord affirmed its divine origin and demonstrated His own involvement in it. This served as a source of great comfort, both for the apostles themselves and for those who would receive this message throughout the nations of the earth. It was a testament to the authenticity and significance of this divine embassy.

The apostles faced immense challenges, toiling with unwavering dedication, bearing heavy burdens, engaging in perilous work, and ultimately sealing their preaching with their own blood. It was crucial for them to possess unwavering certainty that their labor was not in vain or devoid of purpose, but rather brimming with divine power. Amidst afflictions, adversities, and imminent dangers, they needed the assurance that they were engaged in God's work. In the face of a hostile world that opposed them, they required the knowledge that God was on their side. Though they lacked the physical presence of Christ, the very source of their teaching, on Earth, they understood that He resided in heaven, confirming the truth of their proclamation.

Furthermore, it was imperative to provide the audience with undeniable testimony that this teaching did not originate from the apostles themselves, but from God Almighty. It was crucial to emphasize that this message did not stem from earthly sources but emanated from the heavens. Human capabilities alone could not facilitate the forgiveness of sins, the assurance of eternal life, or the proclamation of salvation. Therefore, Christ Himself attested that in the preaching of the gospel, the apostles were mere instruments through which He spoke and made promises. The remission of sins they proclaimed was God's genuine pledge, and the damnation they warned against was God's definite judgment. This testimony remains steadfast for all eternity, assuring us that the gospel, regardless of the preacher, is the very utterance of God. It is proclaimed from His heavenly throne, inscribed in the book of life, and ratified and confirmed in the heavenly realms.

Hence, we come to understand that the power of the keys is simply the preaching of the gospel. In truth, it is not an authoritative power bestowed upon individuals, but rather a divine ministry entrusted to them as stewards of God's Word. Christ did not grant this power exclusively to human beings, but to His Word, through which He has appointed individuals as ministers.

Let us now turn our attention to another passage, which we must interpret in a distinct manner. In the Gospel of Matthew, it is written: "If one of your brothers does not want to listen to the church, let him be to you like a gentile and profane person. Truly, truly, I tell you that all that you have bound on earth will be bound in heaven, and what you have loosed will be loosed there." (Matt. 18:17- 18). However, we should not regard these two passages as completely dissimilar, for they bear a significant resemblance and share a great affinity. Both passages speak in general terms, highlighting the same authority of binding and loosing, grounded in the word of God. They possess a common commandment to bind and loose and convey the same promise.

Nevertheless, there is a distinction between them. The first passage specifically relates to preaching, to which the ministers of the word are ordained. It centers on the proclamation of the gospel and the authority bestowed upon those who minister in its name. The second passage, on the other hand, encompasses the realm of church discipline, particularly the act of excommunication, which the church is permitted to exercise. When the church excommunicates an individual, it is symbolically binding that person, signifying a judgment upon their life and conduct, and serving as a warning of the potential consequences of their actions. It is not an act of condemning them to eternal destruction and perpetual despair. Conversely, when the church receives someone into its communion, it is symbolically loosing them, welcoming them into the fellowship and unity that is found in Jesus Christ.

Therefore, we can discern that the power of binding and loosing operates in both realms, intertwining the realms of preaching and discipline. Through the word of God, ministers exercise this authority in preaching the gospel and proclaiming God's forgiveness. Similarly, the church exercises this power through its disciplinary actions, discerning right from wrong, warning of potential damnation, and embracing those who repent and seek reconciliation. In both cases, the power of binding and loosing is derived from the unity between the earthly and heavenly realms, as God's divine plan is enacted through the ministry of the church.

So, in order to dispel any notion that the judgment of the church is a trivial matter or a mere human opinion, our Lord Himself testifies that such a judgment is nothing less than the proclamation of His divine verdict. He assures us that whatever the faithful pronounce on earth will be ratified in heaven. The faithful possess God's Word, by which they discern and judge the wicked and perverse, and it is through that same Word that they extend grace and reconciliation to those who repent and amend their ways. Their judgment aligns with God's righteous law, which is not a mere earthly opinion but His holy will and heavenly oracle.

Furthermore, it is crucial to understand that when Christ refers to the "church," He is not referring to a select group of clergy with certain outward signs of authority, such as tonsures or shaven heads. Rather, He is speaking of the entire community of faithful believers gathered in His name. Let us not be swayed by the mockery of those who question how one can present a complaint to a scattered and dispersed church. Christ clarifies that He is referring to every Christian congregation, established in various places and provinces.

As He declares, "Wherever two or three are gathered in my name, I am there among them" (Matt. 18:20).

The Spirit, the Word and the Keys

These two passages, as I have briefly and plainly explained, are utilized by those lacking discernment to bolster their arguments regarding confession, excommunication, jurisdiction, and the imposition of laws. They even attempt to derive support for their practice of indulgences. However, if I were to cut through these matters with one stroke, I would deny their claim that their priests are true vicars or successors of the apostles. Nonetheless, the examination of this matter shall be addressed separately in due course.

It is quite amusing to see how they confidently arm themselves with these claims, believing they can use them to fortify their position. However, they fail to recognize a crucial point: Christ did not grant His apostles the power to bind and loose until He had poured out the Holy Spirit upon them. Therefore, I firmly deny that the power of the keys is suitable for anyone except those who have received the Holy Spirit. It is absurd to think that one can wield the keys without the guiding and governing presence of the Holy Spirit, who instructs and directs their actions. While they may boast of having the Holy Spirit, their actions prove otherwise, unless, of course, they consider the Holy Spirit to be something trivial and inconsequential, as they seem to imply. But their claims hold no weight, for people do not place their trust in them.

Their entire scheme crumbles when examined closely. Regardless of the door they claim to have the keys to unlock, we must always question whether they possess the Holy Spirit, who is the true Director and Moderator of the keys. If they dare to claim that they have the Holy Spirit, we must then ask them: Can the Holy Spirit fail? Although they may not openly confess it, their teachings indirectly admit to this truth. Thus, we must conclude that no priests possess the power of the keys. They whimsically and without discernment bind those whom our Lord intended to set free and release those whom He intended to bind. Their claims are nothing but a façade, lacking any true foundation.

It is quite amusing to witness their desperate attempts to justify themselves when confronted with clear evidence that they haphazardly bind and loose without discrimination. They try to assert that they possess the power even without the necessary knowledge. While they do not dare deny the importance of learning for its proper use, they conveniently teach that the power is granted even to those who administer it poorly. However, since the power lies in the statement, "what you bind or loose on earth will be bound and loosed in heaven," either Jesus Christ's promise is false or those who are entrusted with this power should bind and loose as they ought to. They cannot twist the meaning by suggesting that Christ's promise is limited based on the deserving or undeserving nature of the individual.

We also affirm that no one can be bound or loosed unless they deserve it. Yet, the messengers of the gospel and the church possess God's word to determine this worthiness. Through this word, the messengers of the gospel can promise the forgiveness of sins in Christ by faith to all who embrace Him, and they can declare damnation upon those who reject Him. In this word, the church proclaims that those who engage in immorality, adultery, theft, murder, greed, and sinful acts have no share in the kingdom of God, and it can firmly restrain them with strong bonds. Likewise, through this same word, the church can release those whom it comforts when they genuinely repent.

But what kind of power is it if one does not know what is to be bound or loosed? How can one bind or loose without knowledge? Then, why do they claim to grant absolution by an authority supposedly granted to them when the absolution itself is uncertain? What purpose does this imaginary power serve when its effect is nonexistent? These questions expose the flaws in their claims and render their supposed power meaningless.

It is quite amusing to observe their feeble attempts to defend the efficacy of their usage, which can be regarded as nothing more than null or, at best, extremely uncertain. They themselves admit that the majority of priests do not properly wield the keys, while acknowledging that the power of the keys is ineffective when not used lawfully. In light of this, who can guarantee that the one who absolves me has indeed employed the keys correctly? If the priest is inadequate, all I receive is a whimsical absolution that goes something like this: "I am unsure of what should be bound or loosed in you, as I have no grasp of the keys. However, if you deserve it, I absolve you." Such an absolution holds as much weight as if it were uttered by anyone else—be it a layperson (although mentioning that might upset them) or even a Turk or a devil. Essentially, it amounts to saying, "I lack the sure and certain Word of God, which serves as the reliable guide for binding and loosing. Nevertheless, I possess the authority to absolve you if you happen to be deserving."

Clearly, their aim becomes evident when they assert that the keys encompass the authority to distinguish and the power to carry out their decisions, with learning acting as a mere counselor for proper usage. In their disorder and licentiousness, they seek to reign without God and without His Word, discarding the need for divine guidance and making themselves the ultimate arbiters of absolution. How audacious and misguided they are in their attempts to operate without the foundation of God's authority and His infallible Word.

It is quite amusing to witness their attempts to adapt their keys to fit various doors and locks, as if these keys possess a universal jurisdiction that can be applied to confessions, decrees, excommunications, and who knows what else. Allow me to provide a concise explanation for this matter.

When we consider Christ's command to His disciples in the Gospel of St. John, where He grants them the authority to loose or retain sins (Jn. 20:23), it is important to note that He is not appointing them as legislators, officials, copyists, or even humble petitioners. Instead, He bestows upon

them a special testimony, honoring them as ministers of His Word.

Similarly, in the Gospel of St. Matthew, when Christ grants His Church the power to bind and loose (Matt. 16:19), He is not instructing them to excommunicate the poor souls who are unable to satisfy their creditors based on the authority of some mitered and horned figure, accompanied by the extinguishing of candles and the ringing of bells. Rather, He desires that the waywardness of the wicked be reformed through ecclesiastical discipline, by the authority of His Word, and through the ministry of His Church.

Let us not be carried away by their fantastical interpretations and convoluted applications of the keys. Instead, let us seek to understand the true essence and purpose of these keys—to bring about the transformation of hearts and the restoration of the fallen, all through the power of God's Word and the faithful ministry of His Church.

Trafficking in Indulgences

It is indeed quite amusing to witness the delusions of these individuals who claim that the keys of the Church involve the dispensation of the merits of Jesus Christ and the martyrs, as if the pope possesses the authority to distribute them through his bulls and indulgences. One cannot help but wonder if these individuals are in greater need of a remedy to purge their minds rather than arguments to convince them.

The refutation of indulgences, which have already been undermined by numerous criticisms, hardly requires an elaborate effort. The very

fact that they have endured and been upheld for so long, even in the midst of great excess and impropriety, serves as a testament to the darkness and errors in which people have been entangled for years.

People are beginning to see through the deception and manipulation of the pope and his indulgence peddlers. They have come to realize that the salvation of their souls has been commodified, with the purchase of paradise being subjected to a predetermined percentage. Nothing is offered freely. Under the pretense of indulgences, people's purses were drained of their offerings, only to witness the wicked squandering of that money on debauchery, vice, and gluttony. Ironically, those who fervently promoted indulgences were often the ones who held them in the greatest contempt.

This monstrous system continued to grow with each passing day, arrogantly raising its head higher and higher. Each day brought forth new seals of papal bulls, eagerly seeking to extract more silver from the pockets of the people. Yet, despite these exploitative practices, people accepted indulgences with great reverence, even worshiping and purchasing them. Only those with greater discernment could perceive that these were deceitful ploys, though they believed there might still be some benefit to be gained from this deceptive game.

Fortunately, as the world has gradually grown wiser, the fervor for indulgences has waned and become increasingly dormant, until it may eventually fade away completely. It is a hopeful sign that people are beginning to reject these manipulative practices and seek a more authentic understanding of their faith.

It is essential to expose the true nature of indulgences, not only as they have been practiced with all their deceit, robbery, and violence, but also to understand them in their proper and better sense, stripped of any incidental characteristics or vices. In truth, indulgences are nothing but a defilement of Christ's blood and a cunning scheme of the devil to divert the Christian people from God's grace and the life found in Christ, leading them astray from the path of salvation.

Consider how Christ's blood could be more shamefully polluted and dishonored than by denying that it alone is sufficient for the forgiveness of sins, reconciliation, and satisfaction, unless its deficiency is compensated elsewhere? The testimony of St. Peter declares that the law and the prophets bear witness that the remission of sins must be received in Christ (Acts 10:43), yet indulgences claim to grant remission of sins through the merits of St. Peter, St. Paul, and other martyrs. St. John affirms that it is Christ's blood that cleanses us from all sins (1 John 1:7), but indulgences twist this truth by proclaiming the blood of martyrs as absolution for sins. St. Paul declares that Christ, who knew no sin, became sin for us, providing satisfaction for sin so that we might become the righteousness of God in Him (2 Corinthians 5:21), while indulgences assign the satisfying of sin to the blood of martyrs. Paul vehemently asserts that Christ alone was crucified and died for us (1 Corinthians 1:13), yet indulgences audaciously claim that St. Paul and others died for us. In another passage, Paul declares that Christ obtained His church by His own blood (Acts 20:28), but indulgences set a different price for obtaining it—the blood of martyrs. The apostle states that Christ, through His oblation, has perfected eternally those whom He sanctified (Hebrews 10:14), but indulgences contradict this truth by asserting that the sanctification achieved by Christ's sacrifice is perfected by the blood of martyrs. St. John reveals that all the saints have washed their robes in the blood of the Lamb (Revelation 7:14), yet indulgences misguide us to believe that we should wash our robes in the blood of the saints.

No Treasury of Merits

Indeed, their blasphemous teachings reach a pinnacle of extreme sacrilege. Let us examine their conclusions: they claim that the martyrs, through their deaths, have served God in excess, accumulating an abundance of merits that can be shared with others. Therefore, the blood of the martyrs is mixed with that of Christ and amassed as a treasure of the church for the remission and satisfaction of sins. They twist the words of St. Paul, stating that he fills up what is lacking in Christ's passion for the sake of His body, which is the church (Colossians 1:24). In essence, they reduce Christ to a mere common saint, barely distinguishable among the multitude of other saints. They leave only His name, while attributing the power of forgiveness, purification, and satisfaction to this accumulation of merits.

Let us consider their arguments, however. They propose that the blood of the martyrs should be shared for the common good of the church, so as not to be wasted. But was it not sufficient usefulness for the martyrs to have glorified God through their deaths? Did they not bear witness to His truth by shedding their blood? Did they not testify, through their contempt for this present life, that they sought a better one? Did their constancy not strengthen the faith of the church and weaken the resolve of their adversaries? I would argue that they gain nothing from this notion if Christ alone is the one who made atonement, if He alone died for our sins, if He alone was offered for our redemption.

It is essential that we uphold the truth that Christ, and Christ alone, is the focus of our preaching, our contemplation, and our reliance when it comes to obtaining the forgiveness of sins, purification, and satisfaction. Let us not diminish His unique and incomparable sacrifice by intertwining it with the merits of mortals. May we cling to the Gospel message that proclaims Christ as our Savior, the Lamb of God who takes away the sins of the world.

Oh, the malevolence with which they twist and corrupt the passage where St. Paul speaks of making up what is lacking in the passion of Christ! How they misinterpret and misapply his words to serve their own agenda! Let us shed light on this matter.

St. Paul is not referring to any lack in the power of redemption, purification, or satisfaction accomplished by Christ's passion. No, he is addressing the afflictions that the members of Christ, the faithful, endure in their mortal bodies. He reminds us that Christ, who suffered in Himself once, continues to suffer daily in His members. What an honor He bestows upon us by considering our afflictions as His own!

When St. Paul mentions suffering for the sake of the church, he does not mean suffering for its redemption, reconciliation, or satisfaction. Rather, he speaks of suffering for its edification and growth. In other passages, he expresses his willingness to endure tribulations for the sake of the elect, that they may attain salvation in Christ Jesus. He willingly bears these burdens for their comfort and salvation.

Let us not misconstrue St. Paul's words as suggesting any lack in Christ's passion with regard to righteousness, salvation, and life. He does not seek to add anything to the magnificent and complete fulfillment brought forth by Christ's passion. In fact, he testifies boldly and eloquently that through Christ, grace abounds to overcome the abundance of sin. It is by this grace alone that all the saints have been saved, not by their own merits, whether in life or in death. St. Peter himself confirms this truth, stating that it is through the grace of the Lord Jesus that we are saved, just as the saints are (Acts 15:11).

Therefore, let it be known that anyone who seeks to establish the worth of a saint anywhere other than in God's mercy insults both God and His Christ. Salvation and the fullness of grace reside solely in God's boundless mercy, not in the merits of human beings. Let us turn our hearts and minds to the magnificence of God's mercy and the surpassing greatness of Christ's passion, for in them we find true salvation and life eternal.

Indeed, why should we spend so much time discussing matters that are clearly abominable and contrary to the truth? It is evident that such monstrous practices should be exposed and rejected without hesitation. And even if we were to ignore these abominations, the fundamental question remains: Who gave the pope the authority to confine the grace of Jesus Christ within lead and parchment, when the Lord intended for it to be proclaimed and distributed through the preaching of the gospel?

Either God's word must be false, or indulgences are nothing but lies. In the gospel, Christ is offered to us with the fullness of heavenly blessings, encompassing His merits, righteousness, wisdom, and grace without any limitations or exceptions. St. Paul bears witness to this when he speaks of the ministry of reconciliation, declaring that we are to be reconciled to God through Christ, who, being sinless, became a sacrifice for our sins so that we might be made righteous in Him.

On the contrary, indulgences take the grace of Christ and confine it to the pope's possession, measuring it out and attaching it to lifeless materials such as lead and parchment, as well as specific places. In doing so, they separate Christ's grace from the living and powerful word of God. This stark contrast highlights the absurdity and falsehood of indulgences.

The Theologians' Doctrine of Satisfaction Rejected

They seem to give great importance to satisfaction, placing it in the third position within the framework of repentance. They go on and on about the necessity of satisfying God for the sins committed, as if abstaining from past wrongdoings and striving to lead a better life were not enough. According to them, various means can be employed to redeem sins, such as shedding tears, observing fasts, making offerings, giving alms, and engaging in other charitable works. They assert that it is our duty to appease God, settle the debt owed to His justice, make amends for our transgressions, and seek pardon through these acts. Although our Lord, in His merciful generosity, has forgiven our sins, they argue that His justice still requires punishment. Ultimately, their viewpoint boils down to this: while we receive forgiveness for our sins through God's mercy, it is supposedly accomplished by the merits of our own works, which are seen as a form of compensation for our transgressions. In this way, they suggest that God's justice can only be satisfied through the offering of satisfactions.

In contrast to such deceitful claims, I present the unequivocal teaching of Scripture on the free remission of sins (Isa. 52:3; Rom. 5:8; Col. 2:13–14; Tit. 3:4–5). What does remission mean if not a gift bestowed out of sheer generosity? A creditor is not said to remit a debt when he acknowledges that the payment has been made to him; rather, it is the one who, without receiving anything, freely and generously pardons the debt who is truly remitting it. And why, pray tell, do they dare resurrect their satisfactions, which have already been thoroughly refuted? What audacity! Did not the Lord declare through Isaiah, "It is I, it is I who wipe out your iniquities for the love of myself, and I will not remember your sins anymore" (Isa. 43:25)? In doing so, did He not openly proclaim that the cause and foundation of this remission stems solely from His own goodness? Furthermore, since the entirety of Scripture testifies that we must receive the forgiveness of sins through the name of Jesus Christ (Acts 10:43), does it not exclude all other names? How, then, do they teach that forgiveness is obtained in the name of satisfactions? And let them not claim that while satisfactions may be the means, it is not in their name but in the name of Jesus Christ. When Scripture speaks of being "in the name of Christ," it means that we bring nothing of our own for remission, that we lay no claim to our own merits, but rather come to it solely through the love of Christ; just as St. Paul affirms that "God reconciled the world to Himself in His Son for love of Him, not counting people's sins against them" (2 Cor. 5:18–19).

I cannot help but anticipate their twisted response, in line with their perverse thinking. They may argue that reconciliation and remission occur only once, at the time of baptism when we are received in grace by Christ. However, if we happen to stumble and fall after baptism, they will insist that we must atone for our sins through satisfactions. According to them, Christ's blood does not avail us unless it is dispensed through the keys of the church. But why am I merely expressing my apprehension? They openly and shamelessly proclaim their impiety on this matter, not just a few of them, but all of their theological schools. Their esteemed teacher, after acknowledging, as St. Peter declares, that Christ has paid the debt of our sins on the cross (1 Pet. 2:24), promptly qualifies and corrects this statement with an exception or counterclaim. According to their doctrine, in baptism, all temporal punishments for sin are remitted, but after baptism, they are diminished through repentance. Thus, they argue that the cross of Christ and our repentance work together for remission. Yet, the words of St. John paint a different picture: "If someone has sinned," he says, "we have an Advocate with the Father, Jesus Christ, and He is the propitiation for our sins" and "I write to you, little children, because by His name your sins are remitted" (1 Jn. 2:1–2, 12). Clearly, St. John is addressing the faithful. By presenting Jesus Christ as the propitiation for their sins, he reveals that no other satisfaction can appease sins against God. He does not say, "God has reconciled you once through Christ; now seek other means to reconcile yourselves!" Instead, he proclaims Christ as the perpetual Advocate who, through His intercession, continually restores us to the grace of the Father. Christ is the perpetual propitiation through which sins are continuously purified. We must remember the timeless words of St. John the Baptist: "Behold the Lamb of God, behold the one who takes away the sins of the world" (Jn. 1:29). It is He, and He alone, who takes them away. He is the only Lamb of God, the singular offering for sins, purification, and satisfaction.

Let us carefully consider two important aspects. First, we must ensure that the honor rightfully belonging to Christ remains fully intact. Secondly, we must provide solace and peace to troubled consciences by assuring them of the pardon of their sins in the sight of God. Isaiah eloquently proclaims that the Father has placed upon the Son "the iniquities of us all, so that through His wounds we may be healed" (Isa. 53:4–6). St. Peter echoes this truth in different words, affirming that Christ carried all our sins in His body on the cross (1 Pet. 2:24). St. Paul teaches us that sin was condemned in the flesh when Christ, for our sake, became sin itself (Rom. 8:3). In other words, when He willingly offered Himself as a sacrifice, all the weight and curse of sin were annihilated in His flesh. Upon Him was laid the burden of sins, accompanied by their curse, divine judgment, and the damnation of death.

In light of these profound truths, we are not to entertain the fables and falsehoods that suggest we can only partake in the power of Christ's death through our own acts of repentance after baptism. Instead, whenever we have sinned, Scripture directs us back to the sole satisfaction found in Christ. Consider the abhorrent teachings of those who claim that God's grace operates solely in the initial remission, but if we stumble thereafter, our works are required to obtain pardon. If such were the case, how could we reconcile these testimonies with the person of Christ? What an immense contrast it is between acknowledging that our iniquities were placed upon Christ for purification and claiming that they are cleansed through our own works! How preposterous to suggest that Christ is the propitiation for our sins, only to demand that God be appeased by our feeble efforts!

If our aim is to grant peace to the conscience, how can it find solace in the notion of redeeming sins through satisfaction? When will it ever find assurance of having fulfilled its satisfaction? It will be trapped in perpetual doubt, constantly questioning whether God is truly favorable towards it. Such a burden will only bring torment and fear. Those who trivialize sin by settling for light satisfactions display a profound disregard for God's righteousness. They fail to grasp the gravity of sin, as we have already emphasized elsewhere. Even if we were to concede that some sins can be redeemed, what can they possibly achieve when burdened by countless transgressions? A hundred lifetimes would be insufficient to satisfy the demands of such sins, even if one devoted every moment to the task.

Mortal and Venial Sins

In their desperation, these theologians seek refuge in a frivolous distinction between mortal and venial sins. According to their twisted logic, the former require great satisfaction, while the latter can be easily cleansed through superficial remedies like reciting the Lord's Prayer, using blessed water, or receiving the absolution of the Mass. Their mockery of God knows no bounds. Despite constantly uttering the words "mortal" and "venial" sin, they fail to grasp their true meaning. They even dare to classify the most heinous sin of all— the impiety and corruption of the human heart—as venial. On the contrary, we declare what Scripture teaches: "the wages of sin is death" (Rom. 6:23) and "the soul that sins shall die" (Ezek. 18:4, 20). These are the clear principles by which we discern good from evil. As for the sins of the faithful, they are considered venial not because they do not deserve death, but because through God's mercy, "there is therefore now no condemnation for those who are in Christ Jesus" (Rom. 8:1). Their sins are not imputed to them; rather, they are wiped away by the unmerited grace of God.

It is no surprise that they would slander this teaching, accusing it of being a mere paradox reminiscent of the Stoics who equate all sins. But their own words betray them, and they can be easily refuted. Let me ask them this: among the sins they acknowledge as mortal, do they not recognize that some are greater than others? Therefore, it does not logically follow that sins are equal, even if they are all equally deadly. Scripture clearly declares that death is the consequence of sin, just as obedience to the law leads to life. The verdict is inescapable: transgression brings about death. They cannot evade this judgment.

So tell me, what escape do they propose to satisfy such a multitude of sins? It may take a day to satisfy one sin, but during that very time, they commit numerous other transgressions. After all, not a day passes without the righteous stumbling and sinning repeatedly. And when they attempt to atone for a multitude of sins, they end up committing even more, plunging themselves into an endless abyss. And mind you, I am speaking of the most righteous among them. Oh, how their confidence in satisfaction crumbles! What are their dreams and expectations? How dare they continue to cling to the notion of satisfaction? Their folly knows no bounds.

Oh, how they strive to free themselves from the predicament they find themselves in! They concoct a clever distinction between punishment and fault, acknowledging that God's mercy forgives the fault but insists that the punishment remains. According to their twisted logic, satisfactions are necessary to appease God's righteous demand for payment in order to obtain the remission of punishment. How fickle they are in their teachings! Now they declare the remission of fault to be free, while in another breath they prescribe prayers, tears, and other preparations as the means to merit it.

But let us turn to the unyielding testimony of Scripture, which directly refutes this distinction. Although I have already presented compelling evidence to support this, I will bring forth even more passages, hoping that these serpents will be so constrained that they cannot even wiggle the tip of their tail. Listen to the words of the prophet Jeremiah, who declares the new covenant established by God in Christ: "He will no longer remember our sins." Another prophet, Ezekiel, sheds light on its meaning when the Lord says, "If the righteous turns away from his righteousness, I will no longer remember all his righteousness. If the sinner withdraws from his iniquity, I will no longer remember all his sins." When God declares that He will no longer remember the person's righteousness, it signifies that He will not consider it for repayment. Thus, not remembering sins means not counting them for punishment. This truth is echoed in other passages: casting sins behind the back, wiping them away like a cloud, casting them into the depths of the sea, not imputing them, hiding them away. The words of Isaiah, Micah, and the Psalms affirm this divine action (Isa. 38:17, 44:22; Mic. 7:19; Ps. 32:1–2).

Oh, how clearly the Holy Spirit has explained His meaning through these expressions, if only we have the humility to listen and be taught! When God punishes sins, He imputes them; when He punishes, He remembers;

when He calls them into judgment, He does not hide them away; when He examines them, He does not sweep them behind His back; when He gazes upon them, He does not wipe them out like a passing cloud; when He brings them forth, He has not cast them into the depths of the sea.

Now let us turn to another passage in the prophet to understand under what condition the Lord forgives sins. He says, "Though your sins are like scarlet, they shall be as white as snow; though they are red like crimson, they shall become like wool." (Isa. 1:18) In Jeremiah, we find these words: "In that day, declares the Lord, 'I will search Jerusalem with lamps, and I will punish the men who are complacent, those who say in their hearts, "The Lord will not do good, nor will he do ill."'" (Jer. 50:20) In brief, when the Lord speaks of tying sins in a sack, folding them into a bundle, or engraving them in steel with an iron point (Job 14:17, 19:24; Hos. 13:12), it undoubtedly signifies His intention to punish sins.

"Ransom" and "Sacrifice"

Therefore, there should be no doubt that the first statements promise that God will not punish the sins He forgives. If we want to comprehend the meaning of these words, we must simply consider the contrary interpretation.

I implore the readers to heed God's word and not rely solely on my own interpretations. What purpose would Christ have served if the punishment for our sins still remained? When we proclaim that in His body He bore all our sins on the cross (1 Pet. 2:24), we mean precisely that He endured the suffering and punishment that our sins deserved. Isaiah vividly expressed this truth when he declared that "the chastisement of our peace was laid upon Him" (Isa. 53:5). What does "the chastisement of our peace" refer to if not the punishment owed to our sins, which we ourselves should have borne before we could be reconciled with God? Christ, through His sacrificial act, delivered us from the very pains of our sins.

When the apostle Paul speaks of the redemption accomplished by Christ, he commonly uses the Greek term "apolytrōsis" (Rom. 3:24; 1 Cor. 1:30; Eph. 1:7; Col. 1:14), which conveys not only the notion of simple redemption as commonly understood, but also the idea of a price and satisfaction that we might call a ransom. Hence, he states in one place that Christ offered Himself as a ransom for us (1 Tim. 2:6), signifying that He willingly became our substitute, bearing the responsibility and serving as the guarantee to fully free us from all the debts of our sins.

Above all, we find a compelling argument in the manner by which the Lord prescribed the expiation of sins in the Mosaic law. In that divine instruction, He did not present a variety of ways for making satisfaction but rather established the sacrifices as the sole means of repayment. He painstakingly enumerated the different sacrifices to be offered, corresponding to the various types of sins. Now, what does this signify? When the Lord did not command sinners to seek satisfaction through their own good works and merits in order to obtain pardon, but rather required them to offer sacrifices for each expiation, it becomes evident that He intends to testify to the existence of only one kind of satisfaction that pacifies His righteousness.

Let us remember that the sacrifices offered by the Israelites were not regarded as mere human works; their value derived from the very source that rendered them authentic, namely, Christ's unique sacrifice. As for the recompense God seeks from us, the prophet Hosea expressed it eloquently in a single word: "Lord, you will destroy all our sins," signifying the remission of sins, "and we will offer you the sacrifices of our lips," representing the satisfaction that is nothing other than heartfelt gratitude (Hos. 14:2).

Punishment and Atonement

But let us humor these theologians as they wield their chosen scriptural testimonies against us. They present the case of David, reproved by the prophet Nathan for his grave transgressions of adultery and homicide, yet receiving pardon for his sins. However, they argue, he was subsequently punished through the death of his son conceived in adultery. From this, they assert the need to redeem our own sufferings and punishments through satisfactions even after the remission of our sins. They bring forth Daniel's exhortation to Nebuchadnezzar to redeem his sins through almsgiving, as well as Solomon's words about the remission of iniquities due to righteousness and charity, a sentiment also echoed by St. Peter. Furthermore, they reference the woman sinner in the Gospel of Luke, whose abundant love resulted in the forgiveness of numerous sins.

How delightfully twisted their understanding of God's ways is! They consistently view His works through a distorted lens. However, had they taken the time to truly discern what should not be disregarded, they would have grasped that God employs two forms of judgment. In the case of David, the correction he received was not an act of vengeance or punishment for his sins, if only they had observed keenly.

Let us delve into the purpose of the chastisements that God, in His wisdom, sends our way to correct our sins. It is crucial for us to grasp their significance and distinguish them from the punishments inflicted upon the reprobate. Therefore, it would not be excessive to briefly explore these matters.

In our understanding, the term "judgment" encompasses all forms of punishment, which can be classified into two distinct categories: the judgment of "punishment" and the judgment of "correction." When God employs the judgment of punishment, He deals with His enemies in a manner that reveals His righteous wrath, aiming to bring about their destruction and utter annihilation. This is when God's punishment is accompanied by His wrath, constituting an act of divine vengeance. Conversely, the judgment of correction does not involve God's anger or a desire to destroy or confound. Therefore, it is not appropriate to label it as vengeance, but rather as admonition and exhortation. While the former corresponds to the role of a judge, the latter aligns with the heart of a loving father. When a judge punishes a wrongdoer, the punishment befits the sin committed, for it is a reflection of the malevolence displayed. On the other hand, a father, when correcting his son, seeks not vengeance for his transgressions but endeavors to teach him and foster greater vigilance for the future.

St. Chrysostom, in his own unique manner, presents a parable that elucidates this distinction, ultimately arriving at the same conclusion. He states, "The son is beaten, like the servant; but when the servant is beaten, he is punished because he has sinned, receiving his just deserts. The son is chastised with compassionate discipline." Hence, the chastisement of a son serves the purpose of guiding him towards amendment and leading him back to the right path, while the servant receives the consequences he deserves due to the master's righteous indignation.

God's Wrath vs. God's Correction

To facilitate our understanding, let us establish two key distinctions. Firstly, whenever punishment is wielded for the sake of vengeance, it reveals God's wrath and curse—a disposition that He never directs towards His faithful. Conversely, correction serves as a manifestation of God's blessing and a testament to His love, as the Scriptures affirm (Job 5:17–18; Prov. 3:11–12; Heb. 12:5–6). This disparity is frequently acknowledged. The afflictions experienced by the wicked in this world merely serve as a gateway and precursor to the depths of hell, offering them a foretaste of their eternal damnation. Tragically, they remain obstinate and fail to derive any meaningful benefit from such chastisements. Instead, the Lord uses these afflictions to prepare them for the unfathomable suffering that awaits them. In stark contrast, when the Lord chastises His servants, it is not to consign them to death. Rather, the blows of His rod are administered for their instruction and refinement (Ps. 118:18; 119:67, 71). Consequently, the faithful have historically endured such chastisements with patience and a tranquil spirit. Conversely, they have been struck with terror when faced with punishments that clearly manifest God's wrath. Jeremiah beseeches the Lord, saying, "Chastise me, Lord, but let it be for my improvement and not in your wrath, lest I be crushed. Pour out your fury on the nations who do not know you, and on the kingdoms that do not call upon your name" (Jer. 10:24–25). David echoes this sentiment, entreating, "Lord, do not rebuke me in your anger or discipline me in your wrath" (Ps. 6:1; 38:1). It is worth noting that references to the Lord's anger towards His servants when He punishes them and corrects their faults do not contradict this understanding. Isaiah declares, "I will give thanks to you, Lord, for though you were angry with me, your anger turned away, and you comforted me" (Isa. 12:1). Habakkuk likewise states, "In wrath, remember mercy" (Hab. 3:2). Furthermore, when it is said that God profanes His inheritance (Isa. 42:24; 47:6), we must recognize that it does not pertain to God's will or His purpose in chastising His own. Rather, it speaks to the profound sorrow experienced by all those who encounter His strictness and severity.

Indeed, it is through His divine wisdom that God, at times, pricks His servants with mere goads, while on other occasions, He wounds them to the very core, causing them to feel as if they stand at the precipice of hell. In doing so, He warns them that they have incurred His wrath, yet simultaneously assures them of His abundant mercy, surpassing even His strictness. The covenant that He established with Jesus Christ and His followers remains steadfast, for He has pledged that it shall never be broken. Hear His words: "If your children forsake my law and do not walk in my righteousness, if they violate my statutes and do not keep my commandments, I will punish their transgressions with the rod and their iniquities with stripes, but I will not remove my steadfast love" (Ps. 89:30–33). Moreover, to provide us with utmost certainty, He emphasizes that the rods with which He chastises us are of human origin (2 Sam. 7:14). By this illustration, He reveals His intent to treat us with gentleness and kindness. Thus, those whom He strikes with His hand can find no refuge, for they would be utterly confounded and lost. This gentleness, which He consistently demonstrates towards His people, is also articulated by the prophet: "I have tried you in the furnace of affliction, but for my own sake, for my own sake, I do it, for how should my name be profaned? My glory I will not give to another" (Isa. 48:10). This signifies that although the tribulations He sends to purify His people from their vices, He tempers them, ensuring they are not excessively severe.

Let us delve into another crucial distinction—one that illuminates the varying purposes of God's chastisements. When the wicked are scourged by the whips of God in this world, they begin to taste the severity of His judgment. Though they remain unpardoned, having failed to heed the warnings of His wrath, their punishment serves not to correct them but solely to impress upon them the reality of a just Judge who will not allow them to evade their just deserts. In stark contrast, the faithful are disciplined not to appease God's wrath or to satisfy His judgment, but rather to yield fruit through repentance and a return to the path of righteousness. These chastisements, we observe, are more concerned with the future than with the past. Allow me to borrow the words of St. Chrysostom, who aptly states: "The Lord, in punishing us for our sins, seeks not retribution but rather to instruct us for the future." In light of this distinction, we perceive that when Saul was stripped of his kingdom, it was punishment, but when David lost his son, it was correction intended to prompt him toward amendment. Similarly, the words of St. Paul resonate with wisdom: "But when we are judged by the Lord, we are disciplined so that we may not be condemned along with the world" (1 Cor. 11:32). These afflictions that befall us are not intended to shame us but to guide us.

St. Augustine, too, echoes our sentiments when he discerns a profound disparity in the chastisements meted out by our Lord upon His elect and the reprobate. He asserts, "For the elect, these are exercises once they have received grace; for the reprobate, they are condemnations devoid of grace." Citing the examples of David and others, he affirms that our Lord's chastisements aim solely to cultivate humility within His chosen ones. Let us not misconstrue Isaiah's proclamation that "the iniquity of the Jewish people is pardoned, for they have received double for all their sins" (Isa. 40:2) as implying that the remission of sins hinges upon the chastisements we endure. Rather, Isaiah's words convey the message that God, having exacted sufficient punishment and afflicted them profoundly, now invites their hearts to be revived and filled with joy through the proclamation of His merciful grace.

Amidst the bitter trials that befall the faithful, it becomes imperative for them to embrace a particular contemplation: "For it is time for judgment to begin with the household of God; and if it begins with us, what will be the outcome for those who do not obey the gospel of God?" (1 Pet. 4:17). How would the faithful endure their afflictions if they perceived them as manifestations of God's retributive wrath? If one being struck by the hand of God considers Himself the target of a vengeful Judge, it becomes impossible for him to fathom that God is not wrathful and hostile toward him. Consequently, all he can do is view God's rod as a curse and damnation. In essence, those who believe that God's will is to continue punishing them will never be able to convince themselves of His love. However, we can only derive benefit from His discipline if we understand that He is indeed displeased with our vices, yet still maintains a favorable disposition toward us—bearing within Himself a profound love for His children. Whether suffering is eternal or temporal, it matters not; be it wars, famines, plagues, or illnesses, these are all manifestations of God's curses, just as the judgment of eternal death, when our Lord employs them as instruments of His wrath and vengeance against the wicked.

God's Free Pardon is Free

Let us delve into the purpose behind God's correction of David, for it is an enlightening lesson. The correction was not aimed at exacting retribution from David to repay his sin, but rather to impart a profound understanding of God's displeasure towards the gravity of adultery and homicide. By revealing His anger against such acts, God sought to caution David against ever daring to commit such transgressions again in the future. Similarly, we must contemplate the purpose behind God's affliction of the Jewish people with a dreadful plague due to David's disobedience in conducting a census (2 Sam. 24:1, 15ff). Although David was pardoned for the offense, God, in His wisdom, utilized the chastisement as both an example for all ages and a means to humble David. The Lord disciplined him sternly with His rod. This aligns with the universal curse pronounced upon humanity, wherein the miseries we endure—despite having received grace—are reminiscent of the consequences Adam faced for his transgression (Gen. 3:16–19). Through these trials, the Lord warns us about the severity of transgressing His law. Thus, humbled and awakened to our own poverty, we are compelled to yearn ardently for true blessedness.

Should someone claim that the calamities we endure in this mortal life are mere retribution for our sins, it would befit us to deem them lacking in understanding. St. Chrysostom, it appears, shared a similar sentiment when he wrote, "If God chastises us with the intention of preventing us from persisting in wickedness or remaining hardened when He guides us towards repentance, then punishment is no longer necessary." Accordingly, God administers correction with discernment, tailoring His approach to suit the nature of each individual. Yet, as all of us invariably go astray and stand in need of chastisement, our compassionate Father, who seeks our ultimate welfare, visits His corrective rods upon us without exception.

It is quite astonishing how these theologians fixate on a single example like David and remain unmoved by the multitude of instances that clearly demonstrate the free remission of sins. Consider the publican who descended from the temple justified (Luke 18:14)—no punishment pursued him. When St. Peter sought forgiveness for his transgression (Luke 22:62), St. Ambrose astutely observed, "We read about his tears; we read nothing about satisfaction." And let us not forget the paralytic who was told, "Rise, your sins are forgiven" without any imposition of punishment (Matthew 9:2). Scripture abounds with absolutions that are unequivocally depicted as freely given. Therefore, it is from this plethora of examples that we should derive our rule, rather than focusing solely on isolated cases with peculiar circumstances.

Let us examine the exhortation delivered by Daniel to Nebuchadnezzar, urging him to redeem his sins through acts of justice and compassion for the poor (Daniel 4:27). It is essential to note that Daniel did not intend to convey that justice and mercy served as propitiatory offerings to appease God or secure deliverance from punishment. The sole ransom ever accepted was the precious blood of Christ. Rather, when Daniel speaks of redemption, he addresses it in relation to people rather than God. It is as if he were saying, "Oh King, you have wielded an unjust and oppressive rule; you have oppressed the weak, exploited the impoverished, and treated your subjects wickedly. Therefore, in recompense for your unjust actions, extend mercy and justice to your people."

Let us not be swayed by a singular example while neglecting the broader tapestry of evidence that portrays God's gracious remission of sins. The multitude of instances in which forgiveness is bestowed freely should guide our understanding, reminding us of the immeasurable mercy that flows from our compassionate Lord.

In the same vein, when Solomon declares that a multitude of sins are covered by love or charity, he is not suggesting that they are concealed before God, but rather among people. Let us consider the complete sentence: "Hatred stirs up strife, but love covers all offenses" (Proverbs 10:12). Solomon, in his customary manner of contrasting opposites, juxtaposes the destructive outcomes of hatred with the fruitful effects of love or charity. The underlying message is clear: Those who harbor hatred engage in acts of violence, accusation, and insult, fostering a climate of vice and reproach. On the other hand, those who genuinely love one another choose not to focus on faults, but rather to endure and rectify them through gentle admonishment, rather than exacerbating them through constant criticism. It is crucial to understand that this comparison pertains to human relationships and interactions, not to the forgiveness of sins before God. Therefore, let us not cast doubt upon the integrity of St. Peter when he quotes this passage in the same context (1 Peter 4:8). Similarly, when Solomon affirms that our sins are forgiven through mercy and acts of kindness (Proverbs 16:6), he does not imply that they are expiated before God, leading Him to remit the punishments that He would otherwise inflict upon us. Instead, following the common language of Scripture, Solomon signifies that God bestows His favor upon all those who abandon their sinful ways, turning to Him in holiness and producing good works. In other words, he suggests that God's anger subsides and is appeased when we cease from evil. We have delved into this manner of speaking in detail in other discussions.

Explanation of Luke 7:36

Regarding the passage in St. Luke (Luke 7:36ff), those who approach it with discerning judgment and a sound mind will find no cause for disagreement. In this account, the Pharisee secretly questioned our Lord's ability to discern the woman's sinful state, assuming that if He truly knew her, He would not have allowed her to approach Him so readily. Consequently, the Pharisee concluded that Jesus could not be a prophet since He seemed susceptible to deception. To illustrate that the woman was no longer defined by her sins due to their forgiveness, our Lord presented a parable: "A moneylender had two debtors; one owed him fifty francs, the other owed five hundred. He graciously forgave the debt of both. Now, which of them will love him more?" The Pharisee responded, "Certainly, the one who had the greater debt forgiven." To this, our Lord replied, "You have judged rightly. Therefore, consider that this woman, who has shown great love, is a testament to the forgiveness of many sins." It is evident from these words that our Lord did not attribute the remission of sins to the woman's love. Rather, He used her love as a visible confirmation, drawing a parallel to the debtor who was forgiven the larger sum. Thus, we must interpret these words within the context of the parable: "You perceive this woman as a sinner, but you should acknowledge her as transformed because her sins have been forgiven. Her love serves as an outward manifestation of the forgiveness she has received, a means by which she expresses gratitude for the goodness bestowed upon her." This line of reasoning employs an argument of consequences or consistency, whereby we establish a truth through the signs that accompany it. Ultimately, our Lord openly testifies to the means by which the sinner obtained pardon for her sins: "Your faith has saved you." Hence, it is through faith that we receive forgiveness, and through love or charity, we offer gratitude and acknowledge the generosity of our Lord.

The Doctrine of Satisfaction in the Early Church

I must confess that the statements found in the writings of the early church fathers regarding satisfaction do not greatly trouble me. Frankly speaking, it seems to me that many of them, and practically all those whose works have come to our attention, either lacked understanding on this matter or expressed themselves too harshly. However, I am not inclined to believe that even if they were indeed ignorant or simple, they intended their words about satisfaction to be understood in the same manner as the modern proponents of satisfaction do. Take, for instance, the words of St. Chrysostom: "When one seeks mercy, it is so that he may escape examination for his sin, so that he may be spared the severity of justice, so that all punishment may cease. Where there is mercy, there is no more Gehenna, no more scrutiny, no severity, no punishment." No matter how much they may attempt to twist these words, they can never be reconciled

with the teachings of the scholastics on satisfaction. Furthermore, in the book attributed to St. Augustine titled "On Ecclesiastical Dogmatics," it is stated in the fifty-fourth chapter: "The satisfaction of repentance is to remove the causes of sin, not to yield to sin's suggestions." This clearly indicates that in the time of St. Augustine, the notion of repaying past sins through satisfaction was rejected. Instead, every act of satisfaction was seen as a means of guarding against future transgressions and refraining from evil. I will not even mention what St. Chrysostom says, that the Lord requires nothing from us except that we confess our sins before Him with tears, as such sentiments are frequently echoed by the early church fathers. And indeed, in one place, St. Augustine refers to the works of mercy toward the poor as remedies to obtain pardon from God. However, to prevent any confusion or misinterpretation, he further explains his statement in another passage: "The flesh of Christ is the true and singular sacrifice for sins, not only for those forgiven in baptism but also for those that occur afterward due to the frailty of the flesh. These sins, for which the church daily prays 'forgive us our debts,' are indeed forgiven through this unique sacrifice."

It is quite amusing to observe how the early church fathers often referred to "satisfaction" not as a repayment rendered to God, but rather as a public declaration. This declaration was made by those who, after being corrected through excommunication, sought to re- enter the communion of the church and demonstrate their genuine repentance to the community of believers. They would observe certain fasts and engage in other practices to signify their sincere remorse for their past lives, or perhaps to erase the memory of their wickedness. This act of "satisfying" was not aimed at appeasing God, but rather the church itself. The confessions and acts of satisfaction employed in modern times are derived from this ancient custom, albeit in a twisted and distorted manner. These practices have been so corrupted that even their original essence is hardly recognizable.

Now, I am aware that the early church fathers occasionally spoke rashly, as I mentioned earlier. I do not wish to deny that they may have had their moments of failure. However, their works, though slightly blemished, are now utterly tainted when handled by these wild boars. When it comes to arguing from the authority of the early church fathers, I am curious to know whom these proponents of satisfaction will present to us. The majority of the quotations found in their leader Peter Lombard's book are nothing more than the fantastical musings of deluded monks, falsely attributed to saints such as Ambrose, Jerome, Augustine, and Chrysostom. Lombard draws extensively from a book called "On Penitence," which was haphazardly stitched together by an ignorant individual using excerpts from both reputable and dubious authors, and is conveniently credited to St. Augustine. However, it is the type of book that any moderately educated person would be ashamed to associate with their own name.

Satisfaction and Purgatory

Now, let us address the tiresome matter of purgatory, which, with a swift stroke, is severed, overturned, and laid bare by this axe of truth. There are some who suggest that we should simply avoid discussing purgatory altogether, claiming that it only stirs up trouble and yields little edification. While it may seem appealing to cast aside such trifling issues, the consequences are far too significant to ignore. Purgatory, you see, is not merely a concoction of absurdities; it is currently propped up by even greater abominations and has become a stumbling block of considerable magnitude. So, it is hardly advantageous to pretend otherwise.

One could play along for a while, pretending that purgatory was conceived by sheer madness and audacious presumption, without any foundation in the Word of God. Perhaps it was born out of dubious revelations, cunningly contrived by the trickery of Satan. Maybe certain passages in Scripture were wickedly distorted to lend support to this concoction. Although our Lord considers it no trivial offense that human presumption rashly ventures into the secrets of His judgments, strictly forbidding us to consult the dead for answers (Deut. 18:11) and warning against scorning His voice, and He certainly does not allow His Word to be treated so irreverently, we might be inclined to tolerate such things for a time, dismissing them as insignificant.

However, when the purification of sins is sought elsewhere other than in Christ, when satisfaction is transferred to something other than Him, it becomes perilous to remain silent. To separate the purging of sins from the all-sufficient work of Christ is to veer dangerously off course. It is time to confront this deviation and shed light on the truth.

Let us raise our voices and proclaim with conviction that purgatory is a treacherous illusion devised by Satan himself. It not only gravely insults the boundless mercy of God but also renders the cross of Christ utterly meaningless. Purgatory shatters and annihilates our faith, leaving it in ruins. What is their purgatory but a punishment that souls supposedly endure to atone for their sins? Yet, if we strip away the fallacy of satisfaction, their entire purgatorial construct crumbles to the ground.

Now, considering what we have previously established beyond any doubt, that the blood of Christ alone serves as the purification, offering, and satisfaction for the sins of the faithful, what more need be said? Purgatory stands exposed as a grotesque and blasphemous affront to Jesus Christ. I shall not delve into the multitude of lies and sacrileges that are perpetuated to uphold and defend purgatory, nor shall I elaborate on the stumbling blocks it introduces into our religious practices. Suffice it to say that this source of impiety has spawned innumerable evils, casting its dark shadow over the hearts of many.

Purgatory Not in Scripture

Let us now turn our attention to the flawed arguments of these theologians who falsely claim certain scripture passages to support their erroneous beliefs. They assert that when the Lord proclaims that the sin against the Holy Spirit will not be forgiven in this world or the next, it implies the forgiveness of some sins in the next world. To this, I must ask: Is it not evident that our Lord is speaking about the accountability for sin in that passage? If that is indeed the case, then it serves no purpose for their purgatory, for they claim that in purgatory, one faces the punishment for sins already forgiven in this mortal life.

However, in order to silence their claims completely, I shall provide a clearer resolution. In His desire to eliminate all hope of pardon for such a detestable sin, our Lord did not merely state that it would never be forgiven. To emphasize the severity of the matter, He employed a division, distinguishing between the judgment experienced by one's conscience in the present life and the final judgment that will be revealed on the day of resurrection. It is as if He conveyed the following message: "Beware of waging deliberate malevolence against God, for such rebellion leads to eternal death. Those who intentionally strive to extinguish the light of the Spirit presented to them will not obtain forgiveness in this life, where sinners are given the opportunity to repent, nor in the last day when God's angels will separate the righteous from the wicked, purifying His kingdom of all stumbling blocks."

Let us now address their attempt to exploit the parable from the Gospel of Matthew: "Come to an agreement with your opponent so that he may not bring you before the judge, and the judge may not hand you over to the officer, and you be thrown into prison. Truly, I say to you, you will never get out until you have paid the last penny" (Matthew 5:25-26). If we accept their interpretation that the judge represents God, the opponent represents the devil, the officer represents an angel, and the prison represents purgatory, then perhaps they may feel victorious. But it is worth noting that in this passage, Christ intended to highlight the numerous perils individuals subject themselves to when they choose to persist in their disputes and legal battles rather than seeking amicable resolution. His aim was to urge us, through this warning, to always seek reconciliation with everyone. Where then, I ask, do they find their purgatory in this parable? In short, let us consider and embrace the passage in its straightforward meaning, and we will find none of the elements they attempt to attribute to it.

Let us now address the argument they present, drawing from the words of St. Paul: "that at the name of Jesus every knee should bow, in heaven and on earth and under the earth" (Philippians 2:10). These theologians confidently assert that by "those under the earth," one cannot be referring to those in eternal damnation, but rather the souls in purgatory. It would be a reasonable argument if the apostle's mention of "bowing the knee" referred to the genuine adoration offered by the faithful to God. However, the apostle is simply teaching that Jesus Christ has received supreme lordship over all creation from the Father. Therefore, what is amiss if by "those under the earth" we understand the devils who will indeed appear before the throne of the Lord to acknowledge their Judge with fear and trembling? St. Paul himself clarifies this prophecy in another passage, stating, "For we will all stand before the judgment seat of Christ; for it is written, 'As I live, says the Lord, every knee shall bow to me'" (Romans 14:10-11). Now, they may counter by pointing to a passage in the Book of Revelation: "And I heard every creature in heaven and on earth and under the earth and in the sea, and all that is in them, saying, 'To him who sits on the throne and to the Lamb be blessing and honor and glory and might forever and ever!'" (Revelation 5:13). I willingly grant them this point. However, let us consider which creatures are being referred to here. It is evident that even those without souls or understanding are included among them. Therefore, it signifies that all elements of the world, from the highest heavens to the depths of the earth, each in their own place, extol the magnificence of their Creator.

I shall remain silent concerning their references to the history of the Maccabees, as I do not consider that book as part of the canonical Scriptures. However, they believe they have found an impregnable stronghold in the words of St. Paul: “If anyone’s work is burned up, he will suffer loss, though he himself will be saved, but only as through fire” (1 Corinthians 3:15). They ask, “What fire could St. Paul be referring to if not purgatory, which cleanses our stains so that we may enter the kingdom of God in purity?” In response, I would like to point out that several early church fathers interpreted these words differently. They understood the “fire” mentioned here to represent the trials and tribulations, symbolized by the cross, through which the Lord tests and purifies His people, cleansing them from all impurities. Indeed, this interpretation appears to be much more plausible than the notion of a purgatory.

However, I must respectfully disagree with this opinion, as I believe I have a clearer and more certain understanding. Let us consider the apostle’s use of metaphors and parables when he refers to teachings concocted by human minds as “hay, wood, and stubble” (1 Corinthians 3:12). The purpose of this parable becomes evident upon closer examination: just as wood is quickly consumed when exposed to fire, these human teachings prove to be utterly frail and incapable of enduring the test. Now, it is widely recognized that this test is conducted by the Holy Spirit. Therefore, in order to maintain the consistency of the parable, the apostle describes the testing process by the Holy Spirit as “fire” (1 Corinthians 3:13). In the same way that gold and silver are more thoroughly tested when subjected to intense heat, allowing their purity to be discerned, the truth of God is further fortified and confirmed in its authority when subjected to spiritual scrutiny. When wood, hay, and stubble are cast into the fire, they are swiftly consumed and reduced to ashes. Likewise, any human inventions that lack the foundation of God’s Word cannot withstand the refining scrutiny of the Spirit and are ultimately annihilated. In summary, if the teachings under discussion are likened to wood, stubble, and hay, which are consumed and vanquished by fire, and if it is only by the Spirit of God that these teachings are destroyed and rendered powerless, then it logically follows that the Spirit is the very fire by which they are tested. This testing is what St. Paul refers to as “the day of the Lord” (1 Corinthians 3:13), employing the scriptural language that signifies the manifestation of the Lord’s presence in various forms. Primarily, His countenance shines upon us when His truth illuminates our

hearts and minds.

We have already established that the fire, as understood by St. Paul, signifies nothing other than the testing conducted by the Holy Spirit. Now let us delve into the understanding of how those who suffer the loss of their work will be saved through this fire. This inquiry will not pose a great challenge if we carefully consider the individuals being referred to in this context. St. Paul mentions those who, in their earnest desire to edify the church, adhere to the solid foundation of faith, yet introduce various elements that are incongruous with it. In other words, they do not deviate from the essential and fundamental tenets of faith, but rather fall into the trap of incorporating human speculations alongside God's revealed truth. Consequently, it becomes necessary for such individuals to experience the loss of their works. This entails the elimination of their own additions, which have been intermingled with the divine Word, rendering them futile and insignificant. However, in the midst of this process, their very beings will be saved. It is important to note that God does not endorse or approve of their errors or ignorance. Nevertheless, through the gracious working of His Spirit, our Lord will draw them back, rescuing them from their misguided paths. Therefore, it is incumbent upon all those who have contaminated the sacred purity of Scripture with the defilement of purgatory to abandon their efforts, allowing their works to crumble and be cast aside.